The Regional Military Histories

EAST ANGLIA

The Regional Military Histories
Editor · Philip Warner

The Regional Military Histories

East Anglia

Norfolk · Suffolk · Essex · Cambridgeshire

Martin Bates

Osprey

Published in England by
Osprey Publishing Ltd, 137 Southampton Street,
Reading, Berkshire

Picture research · Pat Hodgson
Series design · Behram Kapadia

Filmset and printed by
BAS Printers Limited, Wallop, Hampshire
ISBN 0 85045 182 5

To My Parents

Contents

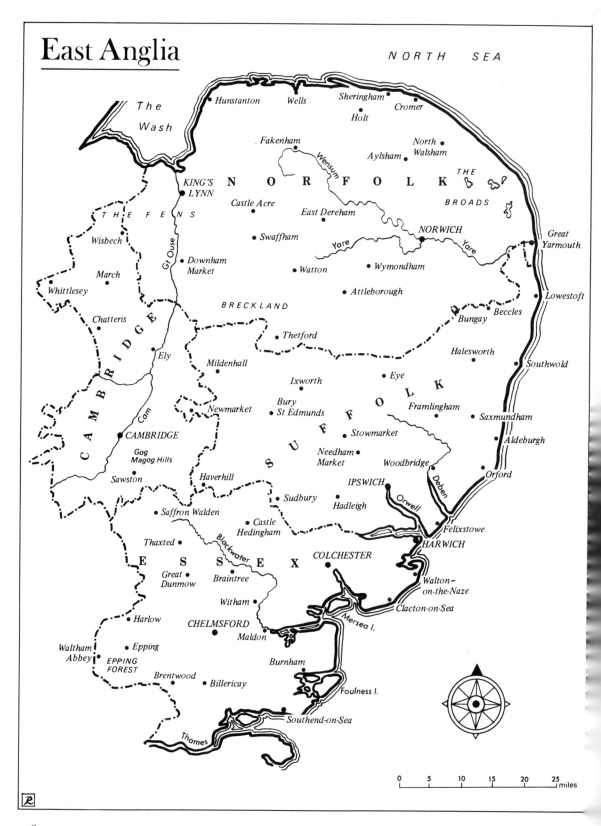

East Anglia

NORTH SEA

The Wash

NORFOLK

THE BROADS

- Hunstanton
- Wells
- Sheringham
- Cromer
- Holt
- Fakenham
- Aylsham
- North Walsham

Wensum

- KING'S LYNN
- Castle Acre
- East Dereham
- NORWICH
- Great Yarmouth

THE FENS

- Wisbech
- Swaffham

Yare

Yare

- Downham Market
- Watton
- Wymondham
- Lowestoft

Gt Ouse

- March
- Attleborough

- Whittlesey

BRECKLAND

- Beccles
- Bungay
- Chatteris
- Thetford
- Halesworth
- Ely
- Mildenhall
- Southwold
- Ixworth
- Eye
- CAMBRIDGE
- Newmarket
- Bury St Edmunds
- Framlingham
- Saxmundham

Cam

SUFFOLK

- Stowmarket
- Aldeburgh
- Gog Magog Hills
- Needham Market
- Woodbridge
- Orford
- Sawston
- Haverhill

Deben

- IPSWICH
- Sudbury
- Hadleigh

Orwell

- Saffron Walden
- Castle Hedingham
- Felixstowe

Blackwater

- HARWICH
- Thaxted
- COLCHESTER

ESSEX

- Great Dunmow
- Braintree
- Walton-on-the-Naze
- Witham
- Clacton-on-Sea
- Harlow
- CHELMSFORD

Mersea I.

- Maldon
- Waltham Abbey
- Epping

EPPING FOREST

- Burnham
- Brentwood
- Billericay

Foulness I.

- Southend-on-Sea

Thames

0   5   10   15   20   25 miles

INTRODUCTION

No visitor to America has any difficulty in finding Civil War battlefields. All those sites are clearly signposted, surrounded by National Parks and, more often than not, dotted with various memorials to the generals and units who took part.

Unfortunately, the same is not true of English battlefields. All too often, all that can be seen is a patch of marsh, a placid meadow, or a sprawling suburb, without so much as a hint that once great deeds were enacted on that very spot. Then again, the tourist in East Anglia will often come across

mystifying features in the countryside; huge mounds, long dykes or stone ruins. Inevitably, the visitor will find no explanation of what these features are, or of how they came to be there.

The purpose of this book is to recount the military history of East Anglia with special reference to the locations of the events. The aim has been to provide the visitor with directions to all the major military sites of the region, as well as to describe the fascinating and bloody history of East Anglia over many centuries.

I

PREHISTORIC EAST ANGLIA

Geography of East Anglia

EVEN a cursory glance at a map shows East Anglia as an unmistakable lump protruding on the eastern side of England. It is clear that East Anglia leads nowhere; that one cannot pass through the heart of our region on the way to somewhere else. That much is obvious at a glance. But a further investigation will show that East Anglia is in fact a peninsula. This is of primary importance in the consideration of early strategic problems.

The geographical situation was not always so. Ten thousand years ago, our island was joined to the Continent. The area of the present North Sea was a land of swamp and fen; it was water from the retreating glaciers after the last Ice Age that flooded over the land to form the present coastline. The English Channel was formed at the same time, separating us from Europe.

This recognizable East Anglian shape can be described easily. To the east lay the sea, which followed the curve of the coastline round Norfolk to form a barrier to the north too. The southern boundary of our region was marked by the Thames – today bridged and tamed, but in prehistoric times an effective obstacle, flanked by dangerous marshes and stretching back into the hinterland of England. The west too was blocked by water. There lay the great natural indentation of the coast, the Wash. South of it stretched the Fens, half a million acres of trackless morass and swamp. Today they are drained and fertile; then they posed an almost insurmountable problem to traveller and invader. They extended much further south in those days – to near the site of modern Cambridge. Thus the only way to enter East Anglia by land was from that gap between Cambridge and the Thames–Lea.

Opposite The Icknield Way at Therfield Heath. The chalk belt, used by traders, settlers and invaders was the only route into East Anglia until the great primeval forests were cleared.

This gap itself was not an easy entrance route because of the nature of the vegetation of prehistoric East Anglia. Vegetation is determined largely by the characteristics of the soil. Basically, East Anglia had three soil belts running roughly north–south, consisting of a central area of very heavy clay with a band of lighter, sandy soil on either side. In prehistoric times, the whole of the southern part of our region was covered by one dense forest. It started at Bow, in central London, extended right up to the Fens, and across all modern Essex to Colchester. In Suffolk, it ran in a great broad belt up the area now known as High Suffolk and on into Norfolk and mid-Norfolk. This area consisted of boulder clay which supported very dense forest which must have been continuous except where the river valleys ran across. This central boulder clay belt forms the watershed of East Anglia; from it, the rivers run to the Wash and the east coast. The Yare, Wissey, Wensum and Nar all rise in this area. Most of the old forest has been destroyed now. Epping Forest is one vestige of it, and there are still fine stands of timber in mid-Norfolk but, generally speaking, we will never know just what the primeval woodland was really like.

To us, woodland makes a pleasant landscape. To prehistoric man it was not so agreeable. It was a source of containment to him because of the difficulties of hacking through the undergrowth, the problem of not getting lost, and the danger posed by the woodland beasts. Further, it was useless land – the kind of soil that supported the trees was a heavy loam which was simply too heavy for the ploughs of the early farmers. Thus, to sum up the role of the early East Anglian forest; it blocked the entrance from the south and formed a barrier to east–west communication across the region.

The lighter soils lie on either side of the clay belt. To the east is an area called the 'Sandlings'. This is an area of open heathland running up the Suffolk coast to Lowestoft. This light soil forms the ten mile coastal strip. It is much changed today through afforestation programmes. The same can be said of the belt on the west side of the clay. Around Newmarket lay a chalk area extending over Cambridgeshire. To the north of this is the Norfolk Breckland, like the Sandlings an area of heathland much changed since the war by the planting of thousands of Scots pine trees. Continuing on up the coast of the Wash, we find the same light sandy soils as far round as Cromer.

To go back to our picture of East Anglia as a peninsula, we see how the neck of the peninsula was closed by the forest, although there was attractive land in Norfolk and on the Suffolk coast. There was one easy corridor through the forest, and this is so important that description of it has been left until last. On the western margin of the central forest lies a corridor of chalk. It is between five and ten miles wide and, as it will not support luxuriant tree life, it forms a pathway of country that is relatively easy to traverse. The chalk ridge is doubly important because it runs from Wiltshire, via Tring and Dunstable, to cross the Thames at Wallingford. From thence it runs to Royston, going through our region by way of Duxford and Pampisford to Newmarket. From there it goes via Kentford to Thetford, then swings north-west to reach the coast near Hunstanton. Thus, not only is this the only feasible route for an invader from the south to take, but it is also the most important land route between East Anglia and the rest of England. The name given to this track is the Icknield Way. It is a name that figures with great importance in the military history of East Anglia.

The Bronze Age

We can begin the story of East Anglia round about 1650 BC. This is the date usually given for the beginning of the Bronze Age, which was to last in Britain for eleven hundred years. This is the period during which the old flint weapons of the New Stone Age began to be superseded by those made of bronze – an alloy of copper and tin which was much stronger than copper alone. Naturally, the new superior weapons were first made in the locations of deposits of copper – like those found in Ireland. East Anglia had no copper deposits so it lagged behind in the production of weapons. Only when a supply of broken weapons (which could be re-smelted) became available could a local industry get under way.

The trading routes for the bronze implements led from Ireland to the Continent by way of Wessex. Wessex at this time was settled by a people who had come from the Low Countries some two centuries earlier. Archaeologists know them as the Bell Beaker folk from their curious drinking vessels. Their settlements lay across the main trading route and they grew wealthy by acting as 'middlemen'. Theirs was a martial society in which the warlords ruled the tribe, and it was also an expansionist society. Soon groups of them began to move up the Icknield Way (the first invaders to use that path)

into west Norfolk. There they formed a ruling caste over the local inhabitants.

The invasion represented a clash between the old Stone Age culture and the new Bronze Age. The most common weapon that the Norfolk people would have had was the stone-hafted axe. Great numbers have been turned up all over East Anglia, and many show signs of having been polished on a block of stone to give a better edge. These weapons existed in abundance, for East Anglia's flint had been systematically exploited for the preceding eight hundred years. The flint mines were at

Grimes' Graves dating from before the Bronze Age, afford a good example of flint being systematically mined for tools and weapons. A diorama at Norwich Museum illustrates the way in which the early miners would have worked.

Grimes' Graves, about three miles north of the modern town of Brandon, on the minor road that connects the A134 and A1065. There are almost 350 mines, ranging from pits ten feet deep to true mine shafts which drop thirty feet and then radiate into horizontal galleries. The total area of the workings is about twenty acres, and the public are admitted

Chalk figure of a pregnant woman found in Grimes' Graves. It may have religious significance connected with the cult of Earth Mother. A crude altar was also found in the mines.

to a number of the shafts, which are in the care of the Department of the Environment.

The new arrivals from Wessex spelt the end of this culture. It was the Wessex people who built Stonehenge, and though there are no monuments of this scale in East Anglia, there have been a number of important finds made in excavations of the graves of these chieftains. The usual method of burial was in a round barrow, surrounded by a ditch and an external bank. A group has been found at Rushford, and there are others at Great Bircham, West Rudham and Weasenham. One barrow at Little Cressingham has yielded up a flat bronze dagger, a grooved dagger with a wooden hilt and a number of gold items. From Rockland All Saints comes a stone mace or sceptre head that must have been the symbol of authority of some chieftain.

Gradually, a unified culture evolved. Archaeologists call this the 'Urn Culture' because it is characterized by the use of clay urns to cremate the dead. In Norfolk and north-west Suffolk, this culture survived right to the end of the Bronze Age. After about 1200 BC a local weapons industry flourished. At Stibbard a hoard of seventy axes and spearheads was found. In Essex a great number of weapons were made that show the influence of Continental styles. The 'carp's tongue' thrusting sword and the winged bronze axehead are both Continental in origin.

The Iron Age

Towards the end of the seventh century BC, East Anglia was raided from the sea by groups of warriors from Belgium. The importance of these raids lay in the fact that the raiders had iron weapons. Like many of man's great advances (such as the cultivation of cereals and the use of bronze) the discovery of iron smelting was first made in the Mediterranean lands. Though its use was known there around 800 BC, it took two centuries for the knowledge to spread into north-west Europe. Iron was much cheaper to use than bronze, and this meant that even simple warriors could afford durable hard-edged weapons. Round about 550 BC, the raiders from Belgium began not just to raid but also to settle East Anglia. Pressure from other tribes on their homelands induced them to make the migration, and it is with their coming that our region moves into the Iron Age.

These first invaders were farmers, and their superior iron agricultural equipment meant that new areas could be brought under the plough. It should be noted that throughout this early period (550–300 BC) there were two quite separate cultures in our region. This can be explained by the fact that the two culture groups came from separate areas of the Low Countries. Those who settled the Breckland had more in common with the settlers of Cambridge and Northamptonshire than with the settlers of the Ipswich area. These latter are closely linked with the people who settled Colchester and the Thames valley.

The northern group, the Breckland one, was to be conquered by a fresh group of invaders over the period 300–250 BC. These newcomers were called the Marnians because they came from the Marne region of France. They penetrated East Anglia in two ways: by sea, from the rivers of the Wash, and overland, from the Thames via the Icknield Way. Their invasion did not go entirely unopposed, and the remains of some of the defences raised by the local chiefs can still be seen. Probably the most important is at Wandlebury, a fifteen-acre enclosure near Cambridge. It lies on the left side of the A604, about two hundred yards past the Little Shelford turning. It has been planted with trees so that there is little of interest to the untrained eye. Originally this was a hillfort defended by a circular ditch and rampart with timber revetment. It measured 1,000 feet in diameter, and was in an extremely strong position. Anyone coming to ford the Cam at Hauxton or Grantchester would have to come close to the fort. The Bourn river and Fulbourn Fen would make a wide detour impossible. Other forts dating from the same period are Tasburgh, South Creake and Narborough on the Icknield Way. Only faint traces of these defences remain.

The Marnians conquered, however, and stayed to form a new aristocracy over the early Iron Age people. Their success was due in no small measure to their superior equipment. Chief among their weaponry was a thing that had not been seen in Britain before – the terrifying horsed chariot. The chariot was common to the peoples of Gaul. One group of relatives of the Marnians, the Parisii (after whom Paris is named), were at the same time colonizing Yorkshire by the use of the chariot. The story of how the horse and chariot developed in the ancient world is interesting. The Egyptians, who built the pyramids about 2500 BC, had not heard of the chariot, which did not appear in their lands for another thousand years. They were introduced there by the Hyksos invaders. The classical Greeks at the siege of Troy (1180 BC) used them, and they were known to the civilization that flourished on Crete around 1500 BC. A thousand years after this the chariot had spread to Britain. Strangely enough, the Romans never used the chariot for warfare.

The importance of the chariot in the culture of the Marnians should not be underestimated. It was common for a chieftain to be buried with his vehicle and ponies. Such a burial has been excavated at Newnham Croft, in Cambridgeshire. Included in this find were the enamelled plates used to decorate the bridles of the chariot ponies. A similar find at Mildenhall was of a body buried with a long iron sword between the skeletons of two ponies.

As we have seen, the Marnians held sway only over Cambridgeshire and the Breckland. The early Iron Age culture (called the Iron Age 'A' culture) went on uninterrupted in the Ipswich region, separated as it was from the Marnians by the great belt of forest. But the Ipswich area too was to be subjugated by the last wave of invaders before the Romans.

The first Roman invasion

On the Continent there lived a tribe called the Belgae. They were Germanic in origin, and spoke Celtic. Round about 110 BC they became involved in a war with the Teutones and Cimbri who were pressing on the Belgic territories in eastern France. Though the Belgae were victorious on this occasion, it soon became obvious that they were doomed to eventual conquest unless new lands could be found. Accordingly, the whole tribe migrated to Britain about 100 BC. They settled in Kent and Hertford-shire, where they became known as the Catuvellauni. This was the migration of a whole people, not just a band of warriors, and they cleared stretches of forest for their farms and built townships of huts defended by ditches and earthworks.

The Catuvellauni soon began to think of expansion, and their eyes turned towards Essex and its Iron Age 'A' people. We know that these people had a tribal name, the Trinovantes, and that their capital was somewhere near modern Colchester. In the course of the war between the two tribes, Cassivellaunus, king of the Catuvellauni, had the father of Prince Mandubracius of the Trinovantes assassinated. Mandubracius, who was evidently losing the war, promptly travelled to Gaul, where he put himself under the protection of the Roman authorities in the person of Julius Caesar. Caesar had long harboured a desire to mount a campaign against Britain, ostensibly because many rebel Gauls had found refuge in our island, but also because he was an extremely ambitious man.

The first Roman reconnaissance of Britain took place in 55 BC. It was a short summer campaign fought in Kent, but it did turn Cassivellaunus' thoughts away from Essex. It became obvious to all the warring tribes that they faced a dangerous common enemy, and they formed a loose confederation with Cassivellaunus as their warlord. The choice was a good one, for Cassivellaunus was a skilful leader.

The next year, 54 BC, Caesar returned. He landed near Sandwich in Kent, pushed inland, and came up against Cassivellaunus for the first time. To Caesar it was a bewildering battle. All day the Romans were harrassed by light horsemen on shaggy ponies supported by skilful charioteers. Whenever Caesar launched a counter-attack, the British faded

Overleaf One of the most remarkable 'mysterious earthworks' in East Anglia. The Iron Age fort at Warham in Norfolk. It was built by the Iceni and used for a short time by the Romans during Bouddicca's rebellion.

away, easily outstripping the encumbered legionaries. This was to be the tenor of the whole campaign. As the days went by, Caesar grew ever more anxious to win the victory that he so badly needed. Then the Trinovantes took a hand.

Mandubracius realized that if Cassivellaunus beat the Romans, the Catuvellauni would be able to swallow up Essex at their leisure. His best policy was to throw in his lot with the Romans, and this he did. As soon as the Romans landed they sent envoys to the Trinovantes offering a mutual non-aggression pact. Mandubracius instantly accepted this and sent a delegation to Caesar's camp. His was not the only tribe to do so. Another party who also made peace were a tribe called by Caesar the 'Cenigmani'. These are the people known to us as the Iceni of Norfolk. They are, of course, the descendants of the Marnians who had conquered the Breckland two centuries earlier.

But to return to the story. The Trinovantian delegation were able to tip the balance in Caesar's favour. In their possession they had vital information that was to change the course of the whole campaign. Quite simply, they were able to tell Caesar the exact location of Cassivellaunus' fort, where the British were assembled. Caesar, harried by a guerrilla war and with his invasion plan crumbling, now had a definite goal to aim for. The site of the fort was in fact at present-day Wheathampstead in Hertfordshire. Brushing opposition on the Thames aside, Caesar's legionaries force-marched north, and Wheathampstead fell to their assault. This was almost the final blow in the war. For although Caesar had to fight a Kentish tribe who had been stirred up by Cassivellaunus, the British knew they were beaten and came to terms. Caesar says, 'I demanded hostages, fixed the annual tribute payable by the British into the Roman treasury, and strictly forbade Cassivellaunus to interfere with Mandubracius and the Trinovantes.' That done, Caesar went back to Rome, never to see these shores again; and Cassivellaunus returned to Wheathampstead to meditate on the Trinovantian treachery and plan his revenge.

Cunobelin and the defeat of the Iceni

A generation was to pass before the Catuvellauni threatened the Trinovantes again. Cassivellaunus was dead, and the new king was called Tasciovanus. We know the names of a number of the rulers of this period because they had recently adopted the Roman practice of issuing coins stamped not only with the king's name but also the place of minting. Careful dating and examination of the pattern of distribution of these coins over a certain area has been a valuable help in the reconstruction of past events.

Tasciovanus succeeded to the throne about 15 BC. He lost no time in attacking Addedoramus of the Trinovantes and gained control of the Trinovantian capital. This success did not last long, for we find Addedoramus' coins scattered over all north-east Essex to the exclusion of those of Tasciovanus. It is quite possible that the latter had his hands full with a war against the Iceni; but more of that later. Addedoramus died about AD 1, and before the Catuvellauni could invade Essex, the Belgae of Kent struck. Under their king Dubnovellaunus, the people of Kent crossed the Thames and seized all of modern Essex. It was this onslaught that first began to change the culture and customs of the Trinovantes' Iron Age 'A' life in the direction of those of the Belgic tribes.

Our next reference to Dubnovellaunus comes from Rome in AD 14, where his name is recorded as being among the refugee suppliants to the Emperor. Luckily, we know something about how he was reduced to this position. Tasciovanus died about AD 10 and was succeeded as king of the Catuvellauni by his son, Sego, who reigned at Verulamium. Tasciovanus also had another son, a far more impressive character called Cunobelin or Cunobelinus. This king is actually the 'Old King Cole' of the nursery rhyme and is also Shakespeare's King Cymbeline. Cunobelin, deprived of the succession to the Catuvellauni throne, took a band of followers to Essex and flung Dubnovellaunus of Kent out. He annexed all of Essex and set it up as an independent kingdom. He took over the old capital near Colchester, refortified it, and gave it the name of Camulodunum – 'the fortress of Camulos the war god'.

Camulodunum is in fact the whole of the peninsula in north-east Essex that lies between the Colne and Roman rivers, an area of about ten square miles. This particular area would have been very attractive to early man. The soil is an outcrop of gravel that would have been easy to work by comparison with the surrounding forested clay. The heart of the peninsula was protected by a series of massive dykes, all of which faced west. The dykes

Opposite This aerial photograph shows traces of the dykes which defended Camulodunum, the capital from which the Belgic dynasty ruled much of southern England.

have been so ploughed up that any pattern is really only apparent from the air today. The very heart of the defences – probably the site of the royal buildings – is itself a minor peninsula formed by the Colne and one of its tributaries. Here, the Colne valley runs up to a flat-topped hill connected by a neck to the main gravel plateau. This site has its own freshwater springs, and just opposite it lies Sheepen Ford, the lowest tide-free ford of the Colne. A dyke protected these inner defences, but again there is not much to see now. The site has largely been spoiled, but if you want to visit the ground from which Cunobelin ruled go to the triangle between the By-pass, Lexden Road and the road to the railway station and you are on the old capital.

From here the aggressive Cunobelin extended his kingdom. First he expelled his brother Sego from the throne of the Catuvellauni, an act which brought the two tribes, Trinovantes and Catuvellauni, under one single dynasty, and marks the end of the Trinovantes as a separate entity. The homeland of the people of Dubnovellaunus was next – by AD 25 the whole of Kent was in Cunobelin's hands. It was the turn of the Iceni next.

There is much that we do not know about this period. There is, for instance, an Iceni coin dating from Tasciovanus' days that was minted at Camulodunum. Does this mean that the Iceni held Essex for a time? We do not know for sure. Archaeology has, however, given us some clues as to the nature of the war. The Iceni were concentrated in Norfolk, and the region on the Icknield Way around Cambridge was their frontier. They set up a number of fortresses to keep the Catuvellauni at bay, and some of these can still be seen today. There were two border fortresses held as advanced posts – Clare on the River Stour and Saffron Walden, situated at an important ford on the Essex River Cam. Clare was quickly lost. The remains of the fort – a double rampart and ditch – lie on the west side of the B1063, just north of Clare. The Iceni were now pushed back to their fort at Saffron Walden. If the loss of Clare had been bad, that of Saffron Walden would have been disastrous to the Iceni cause. For, with the Catuvellauni capital being near modern Colchester, the Catuvellauni could be expected to make great use of the river valleys as being the easiest terrain to penetrate westwards towards the Iceni frontier. The loss of Clare had opened up the route from near Colchester via Sudbury to Haverhill, along the Stour valley. From there, it was only a matter of five miles through the higher country

before the invaders would be in the low plain of the Granta valley, with the Iceni borderland open before them. The loss of Clare had opened this up as an invasion route, although at the head of the Granta valley, just where the invading Catuvellauni would have emerged, there is a place called 'Shudy Camps', where a number of tumuli are located. This

might well have been an Iceni fortress built after the loss of Clare.

The Essex Cam valley was to be the next line of Catuvellauni advance. It was the key to the whole Iceni defences. The Iceni had been expecting trouble from the Catuvellauni since the days of Tasciovanus. Then, the Catuvellauni capital had

The hillfort at Wandlebury was probably built 300–250 BC by local chieftains anxious to prevent the incursions of Marnian warriors. It later became the pivot of the Iceni defence against the Catuvellauni.

been in Hertfordshire and, naturally enough, the Iceni envisaged that the advance would be up the Icknield Way from the direction of Dunstable and Royston. Consequently, they planned their defences to meet this threat. At Royston they raised a dyke with its flanks protected by natural obstacles, while at Fowlmere, four miles farther up the Icknield Way from Royston, they built an incredibly strong fortress complete with wet moat. Wandlebury, the old fortress on the Gog Magog Hills just outside Cambridge, which had been built as a defence against the Marnian invaders who founded the Iceni tribe, was re-occupied and put back into a state of defence after three hundred years of desolation.

The seizure of Essex and the transfer of the Catuvellauni capital there by Cunobelin completely changed the strategic picture. Now, instead of the friendly Trinovantes on their flank, the Iceni faced the prospect of an assault up the Cam valley that would simply by-pass their defences around Royston. It was in an effort to prevent this that the fortress of Saffron Walden was built. Interestingly enough, Wandlebury can be seen from the fort at Saffron Walden. It is certain that observers at Wandlebury could see signal fires from Saffron Walden if the fort there came under attack.

Come under attack it did, and it fell. The fortress lies to the west of the modern town, just off the A11. Over the centuries the site has become afforested, and could be easily missed. Much of the fort has been levelled, but there are still traces of the ditch, which was about fifty feet wide. It was here that the battle that decided the fate of the border country was fought. The Iceni must have looked magnificent in battle array: the chiefs wearing the gold and silver necklets that they loved so much; the leading warriors glinting with bronze amulets and shield decorations; and the chariot ponies splendidly decked out in enamelled bridles and headgear.

That the loss of this battle had very serious consequences for the Iceni is clear from two archaeological finds. One of the main differences

between the Iceni and the Catuvellauni was that the latter were in the habit of cremating their dead. At Snailwell (near Newmarket) and at Elveden (a few miles south of Thetford) the remains of two cremated chieftains have been discovered. The goods found in the graves are similar to finds made at Camulodunum, leaving no doubt that the Catuvellauni were in control of all the Cambridge region as far as Thetford.

From this period following the loss of the frontier, we have evidence of the last defences of the Iceni. Their leading outpost was at Thetford; there they built a fortress whose traces can still be seen in mutilated form as the earthworks round the later Norman castle. Much farther north they built the forts that would serve as a last rallying point against the overwhelming might of the Catuvellauni. At Holkham, the woods north-east of Narborough hide traces of the defences. At Warham, a mile north of the village of Wighton on the River Stiffkey, lies the best-preserved of all the East Anglian Iron Age forts. In the marshes lies a double rampart and ditch enclosing an area of about three acres. It was here that the Iceni planned their last stand.

It was a last stand that they did not have to make. Cunobelin was growing old, and increasingly there were family squabbles to divert his attention. He was forced to banish one of his sons, Amminius, who went to Rome and tried to get the Roman Emperor Caligula interested in an invasion of Britain. Caligula was assassinated in AD 41 before these plans could come to fruition. Almost immediately after, Cunobelin died, to be succeeded by his sons Caractacus and Togodumus who ruled jointly. Trouble was soon on the way for them in the shape of a king called Verica, who had been dispossessed of his throne by their father. He had petitioned the Emperor Claudius for restoration of his kingdom, and this was to provide the ostensible reason for the invasion of Britain by Rome. So even as the Iceni feared that they were doomed, salvation came in the shape of the Roman legions.

2

ROMAN EAST ANGLIA

The Roman invasion of AD 43

IN AD 43, a Roman general named Aulus Plautius was entrusted with the task of conquering Britain. He had command of four veteran legions which were stationed in Germany, and through the early summer months they gathered at the rendezvous at the mouth of the Rhine. From Strasburg came the 2nd Augusta, from Mainz the 14th Germina, from Cologne the 20th Valeria, and from the Danube came the 9th Hispania, under their commander Vespasian, later to become a Roman Emperor.

Since Caesar's foray a century earlier, Rome had never really given up the idea of making Britain part of the Empire. Increasingly, Rome had realized just how rich Britain was as more and more trade routes were opened between Gaul and this island. There were also military reasons for the invasion of Britain. While Caesar had faced a very loose confederation of tribes, united only in the face of common danger, southern Britain was now under the sway of one dynasty, whose capital was at Colchester and who were, the Romans believed, quite capable of mounting an attack on Roman Gaul. In addition, they had an ostensible justification for interfering when Verica, king of what is now Surrey, was turned off his throne by Cunobelinus of Colchester. Verica appealed to the Emperor Claudius to help him recover his throne. Finally, Claudius himself wanted to imitate his imperial predecessors by conducting a triumphant campaign which the invasion appeared to offer.

The invasion fleet sailed in three divisions, and landings were made at three separate but unrecorded places on the coast of Kent. This was the area where Caesar had landed, and it had the strategic advantage of leading to the Thames valley, to the north of which lay Camulodunum, capital of the Catuvellauni, and thus the heart of British resistance. The first battle of the campaign was fought on the Medway, when the Romans managed to make a very difficult river crossing in the face of stiff British opposition.

The Britons, led by Caractacus, fell back to the Thames, and we have two different accounts of what happened next. According to the Roman historian Dio Cassius, the Romans managed to get a force over the Thames, which in those days was lined with marshes. Once across, they were embroiled in a fight with warriors who knew every inch of the land, and the Romans were so badly mauled that they were forced to retreat to the south bank and await reinforcements from Rome. A different story is told by another historian, Suetonius. He attributes the halt to the Emperor Claudius' lust for glory. He pictures Claudius waiting in Rome until the army is on the Thames and then, assured of victory in a march on the British capital, coming to Britain to win cheap glory.

At any rate, Claudius did come, bringing reinforcements with him, including elephants. We have no details of what happened next. All that is known is that the Romans did storm those massive earthworks on the Colne, and the Emperor received the submission of the tribes that he had conquered, and the tribute of those who had no quarrel with Rome, including the Iceni. With that, Claudius returned home, having been in Britain sixteen days.

The Iceni were probably very pleased with what had transpired. They had feared Catuvellauni aggression, and now that threat had been decisively removed by the victory at Camulodunum. The Iceni king, Saemu, offered homage to the invaders, and in return they made him a 'client king', able to run his domestic affairs independently, and having some measure of sovereignty. For their part, the Romans were grateful for the agreement. Plautius was anxious to push inland before going into winter quarters, and the treaty with the Iceni secured the right wing of the advancing Romans. The 9th Legion went north, fighting up into the Humber to establish

Opposite Cassivellaunus and other British princes come to terms with Julius Caesar. Caesar's victory was due in no small measure to the help furnished by the Trinovantes of Essex. Engraving by White after the artist Wale.

Above Caesar's landing on the south coast of Britain. His hopes of a swift and glorious campaign were rudely shattered by the guerrilla tactics of the Ancient Britons.

their garrison at Lincoln. Elsewhere the legions pushed out of Essex until, four years later, the invaders were masters of everything to the south of a line drawn from the Humber to the Severn. The next governor, Ostorius Scapula, advanced the frontier to the Trent–Severn line from the earlier boundary.

Iceni risings against the Romans

By this time the Iceni were beginning to be apprehensive of Roman aims. It probably seemed to them that they had exchanged the threat of the Catuvellauni for that of Rome, finding exploitation and slavery at Roman hands. The last straw, or so the historian Tacitus tells us, was the governor's decision to confiscate the weapons of all those who showed any dissatisfaction with Rome. With that, the Iceni rose. This was in AD 49–50, a small-scale outbreak, easily quelled. The Iceni and their allies, the Coritanii of Lincolnshire, offered battle to the Romans at an unknown site. Apparently, they fought from behind earthworks, so the site may well be the fort at Cherry Hinton, just outside Cambridge. Inevitably, the legionaries won. Once they had stormed the defences, they hacked to pieces everybody they found inside the fortress. The other result of the rising was that the Iceni king, Saemu, was replaced by one Prasatugus.

It was to be eleven years before the full fury of the Iceni was felt. In that year, Prasatugus died. As a client king, he feared that the Romans would not safeguard the succession of the throne to his widow Boudicca (Boadicea, as she has been incorrectly known). Prasatugus was a wealthy man, and in an effort to make sure that Boudicca got the throne, he left half of his fortune to the Emperor Nero, hoping that Nero would thus become well-disposed towards his family. It was a hope that was to be very quickly shattered. Rapacious and corrupt Roman officials moved into the kingdom to secure Nero's bequest. They were ruthless in their treatment of the Iceni.

Boudicca was flogged and her daughters raped, and the discontented Iceni rose again. Boudicca herself led them, a striking, imposing woman with long tawny hair. Her statue, somewhat romanticized, stands outside the Houses of Parliament today.

The Iceni soon found that they were not alone in their struggle. A few miles from old Camulodunum, right in the heart of modern Colchester, a new Roman town was being built. It was not a usual Romano-British township, but a *colonia*, or settlement for retired legionaries. Any man who served with the Eagles for twenty-five years received Roman citizenship (with all the privileges that that entailed) and a grant of enough land to make a comfortable farm. Veterans were settled together in *coloniae*, and Colchester was one of these. Ex-legionaries, naturally, were not the kindest of masters, and thus there was widespread dissatisfaction among the Trinovante serfs who slaved on the land; it was land that had been theirs less than twenty years before. Even the old British nobility hated Rome as much as the slaves did. Their complaint was that they were forced to pay crippling taxes towards the upkeep of a gigantic Roman

Below Caractacus, a prince of the Catuvellauni, led the fight against the Romans. After the fall of Camulodunum he continued the struggle until captured in Yorkshire.

Opposite Bronze bust of the Emperor Claudius found at Saxmundham. Claudius was in Britain for only seventeen days but in that time he crossed the Thames and stormed Camulodunum.

Romano-British bronze helmet found at Witcham, Cambridgeshire. Iron armour and weapons are particularly susceptible to corrosion in the acid soil of East Anglia but bronze survives much better as this example shows.

temple at Colchester, dedicated to the cult of the Emperor Claudius.

It was Colchester that bore the brunt of the Iceni frustration, and there can have been few more bloody episodes in our past. From their homeland in Norfolk, the tribesmen came down towards Colchester, probably taking a route that is closely followed by our A140. As they advanced, they grew stronger as bands of Trinovantes swelled their ranks. In the new town by the Colne, the Roman settlers waited. But there was treachery afoot. Misled by pro-rebel Trinovantian nobles as to the strength and intentions of the insurgents, the defenders raised no fortifications, nor did they even send the women and children to safety. That night, the statue to Victory, raised in honour of the Claudian conquest, fell down for no apparent reason. It was an ominous warning of what was about to take place. When the Iceni attacked they swamped the defence and penetrated right into the heart of the hated city. A few Romans managed to get back to the Temple of Claudius and made their

last stand there. It was a forlorn resistance that was overcome two days later when the tribesmen stormed even this. Then the atrocities began. To the accompaniment of music and sacrificial banquets men and women were mutilated and tortured to death.

From Colchester, Boudicca led her warriors to St Albans (Verulamium) which met the same fate as Colchester. From there, the next target was to be Londinium (London). But before this new Roman trading town could be dealt with, there was one problem which had to be overcome. The 9th Legion at Lincoln had got word of the revolt and were marching south to put it down. Somewhere in our region, at a site that has not yet been discovered, the Iceni set an ambush. Two thousand legionaries under Petillius Cerialis were caught in the trap and surrounded. They were slaughtered almost to a man. Only a few of the light cavalry were able to hack their way out of the hordes of tribesmen. It was at this point that the Romans were closest to losing their new province: the whole of the east coast was in arms, and the garrison at Lincoln had now been wiped out.

Today it is a matter of ten hours by car from Anglesey to Colchester. Then, it took much longer, especially to foot-slogging legionaries. But Anglesey was where the Roman field army was, and so back it came to face the new threat. While the 14th and the 20th tramped steadily back through the mountains of Wales, their commander, Suetonius, rode on ahead with all the cavalry at his disposal. On the way, he sent a message to the fourth of the Roman Legions in Britain – the 2nd Augusta at Gloucester – ordering it south to London. Unfortunately, the Legion commander was on leave, and the Camp Prefect refused to move. The result was that when Suetonius reached London, which was hourly awaiting assault, he had no troops with which to defend it. Few men can ever have faced a decision such as that which Suetonius had to make. He resolved to leave London to its fate and retreat with his few horsemen until the foot soldiers came up. So London, the third city of the south-east, shared the fate of Colchester and St Albans.

But by his decision to turn a deaf ear to the pleas of the citizens of London, Suetonius saved all of England for Rome. For while the Iceni were torturing, looting and burning, the legions were tramping ever closer. Finally, they arrived and Suetonius was ready to give battle to Boudicca. The site of the battle is unknown, although some authorities identify it with Amesbury Banks in Essex. Suetonius

Tombstone of Marcus Savonius Facilis, centurion of the Roman XXth legion. It was found at Colchester where the XXth garrisoned before being moved off to North Wales to conquer the Silures.

drew his men up in a defile with a thick wood behind to protect his rear and open ground in front. In the centre stood the veteran legionaries, flanked by the auxiliaries, and with the cavalry on the wings. Opposing them were the Iceni, who seem to have been a tangled mob of foot, horse and chariots, with their families and a huge baggage train in their rear.

As the day passed, the Romans performed prodigies. Outnumbered as they were by ten to one, they stood their ground, flinging back wave after wave of berserk tribesmen. Time after time the cavalry were forced to charge, wielding lances in an effort to break up the attacks of the Iceni before the legionaries were swamped by sheer weight of numbers. The auxiliaries included archers who proved useful against the dreaded Iceni chariots, firing at the ponies to send animals, chariots, drivers and warriors cartwheeling over in a heap.

At last, with night starting to fall, the advance was ordered. Roman discipline had prevailed and now it was the turn of the legionaries to attack. Trapped by their own baggage train, the Iceni were slaughtered in droves as the Romans came on, knocking down the warriors with their shields, then finishing them off with the deadly short legionary sword. Boudicca poisoned herself, and the defeated crawled home. The Camp Prefect of the 2nd Legion at Gloucester, who had not answered Suetonius' summons, fell upon his sword.

Roman remains in East Anglia from the time of Boudicca

The rebellion of Boudicca was responsible for most of the Roman military remains in East Anglia. There are a number of fortlets, such as those at Great Chesterford, Ixworth and Coddenham, while a little marching camp was built at Wighton. This latter was an Iceni fortress taken over and improved by the Romans. Another place of interest is Thornham in Norfolk. This was the site of a signal station designed to send a warning across the Wash to a similar station in Lincolnshire, behind which was the garrison at Lincoln. Unfortunately, there is little for the casual observer to see at any of these places. They were all discovered by aerial

photography and can really only be appreciated from the air.

This is not true of Colchester, which has some magnificent Roman remains. The castle is the best place from which to start a tour. The Norman keep was built on the foundations of Claudius's Temple. It was here, in the quiet castle park, that the worst atrocities were committed. The castle contains a very fine museum with many interesting exhibits from the Roman age. Both the main street by the castle and the road that runs at right angles to it are the sites of old Roman streets, and in many places archaeologists have found a thick layer of ash in the foundations of Roman sites that marks the passage of the Iceni two thousand years ago. One such place is the church of All-Hallows-in-the-Wall, which is built on the site of some Roman building burned by Boudicca.

The other important remains in Colchester are the walls. Roman Colchester was surrounded by a wall three thousand yards in length, strengthened by rounded bastions. Of the latter, only two remain. The walls are still the best-preserved Roman walls of any town in Britain. Considerable portions survive along one side of the Priory Street car park. Also, nearby, is the famous Balkerne Gate, which was once one of the most splendid gates ever built in these islands. Today it has an extremely forlorn and uncared-for look, and is rather disappointing to the visitor. The walls in fact consist of huge limestone blocks brought from the beach and filled over with bricks and rubble. This method of construction was necessary because of the lack of suitable building stone in our region.

The end of the Roman occupation

After Boudicca's revolt, there was no more trouble in East Anglia. Romanization took place and trade increased, and we have two important walled towns dating from the second century AD. At Caister-by-Yarmouth, in the area formed by the junction of the modern A149 and A1064 can be seen the remains of some walls that were part of a new town founded about AD 125 to trade with the Rhine country. This town was protected by a flint wall ten feet thick. At

Boudicca, Queen of the Iceni as depicted by the engraver R. Havell in 1815. Based on a contemporary historian's description it shows her flowing tawny hair and many-coloured kirtle. It is less successful in conveying the 'terrifying, imperious aspect' of the leader of the Iceni rebellion.

nearby Caistor-by-Norwich some of the defences of the old area capital – Venta Icenorum – are still visible. Originally the defences consisted of a wall twenty feet high reinforced by U-shaped and square bastions, fronted by a ditch eighty feet wide. Access over it at the gateways was by timber bridges.

The military frontier of Roman Britain was far to the north of East Anglia, and was marked by Hadrian's Wall. During the latter part of the third century, Britain was beset by attackers against whom the Wall was no defence. The problem was one of sea raiders: fierce Saxon, Scottish and Pictish pirates who infested the Channel and North Sea,

Burgh Castle, best preserved of the Roman 'Saxon shore' forts. It would have had wide ditches designed to keep the Saxon raiders far enough from the walls for the catapults to be used to advantage.

preying on the fat Roman merchantmen. It was their activities which led to the last series of Roman military building in our region. From the first, the basic Roman strategy underlying operations against the pirates was to intercept them before they could do any damage. That is, they were supposed to be intercepted at sea by ships rather than engaged on land during the course of a raid. Carausius, admiral of the *Classis Britannica*, the Roman fleet based in Britain, soon found a way to make himself rich. Instead of intercepting the pirates on their inward voyage to our shores, he waited until the raid was over and the loot-laden raiders were making for home. Thus when he defeated them, he was able to keep a good proportion of the spoils for himself. When he was accused of this, Carausius did not go to Rome for trial but instead seized Britain and had himself proclaimed Emperor. His 'Empire' survived for six years until his chief finance officer, Allectus, murdered him and reigned in his stead. Allectus was not overthrown for another three years.

The chief interest of all this for us is that the nine year reign of the two usurpers, from 287 to 296, saw the beginning of the system of defence known as the fortresses of the Saxon Shore. On both sides of the Channel are a number of forts, mostly situated on or near river estuaries. On the English side of the Channel, the forts extend from the Isle of Wight to the Wash. There are four in our area. The northernmost was Branodunum (Brancaster) which lay on the approaches to the Wash. It guarded the ferry connection between Holme and Burgh-le-Marsh as well as the rivers leading down into the Fens (much of which had been reclaimed by the Romans and was a fertile grain-growing area) and Cambridge. Gariannonum (Burgh Castle) lay next, guarding the port of Caister-by-Yarmouth from its position at the junction of the rivers Yare and Waveney. Farther south again was Walton Castle (Felixstowe) which stood watch over the estuaries of the Deben and the Stour–Orwell. Lastly, the fortress of Othona stood at Bradwell in Essex on a windy headland at the mouth of the Blackwater.

Of these four, three have all but disappeared. Walton castle has been swallowed by the sea. It stood just off The Dip in Old Felixstowe, and unwary bathers may still catch their feet on its masonry. At Branodunum nothing remains above ground. At Othona there is still one wall about two hundred feet long, though the tiny church which stands across the gateway of the old fort is built of materials from the Roman structure. These disappointing remains are made up for by the splendour of Gariannonum. Three sides of it still remain on a bluff overlooking Breydon Water. They still are fifteen feet high with great thick bases of twelve feet. What is particularly interesting is that the bastions, on which were mounted the heavy *ballistae* or catapults, still survive. The whole fort is about five acres in area. An inscription found at the site tells us that the place was once garrisoned by the Stablesian cavalry, who came from modern Yugoslavia.

Obviously, all these forts were strong enough to resist even the most determined assault. But this was not their primary function. Their role was to act as bases for mixed garrisons of soldiers and sailors who could harry the raiders by sea or by land. Apart from the large fighting galleys there were numbers of light scout craft stationed at the forts. A contemporary description tells us that these were very fast vessels powered by twenty oarsmen. The men were clad in garments of sea-green and the hulls of the boats were also painted the same colour – one of the earliest examples of camouflage. The craft were called *Pictae* because they resembled the Pictish currachs, and their task was to report on the enemy's movements to the Roman fleet. Also, as we have seen, there was light cavalry in the forts to hunt down any raiders who slipped ashore.

It says much for the strategic concept behind the forts that the pirates were held at bay for sixty years. It was in 367 that the raiders won their first great victory. For the first time the Saxons, Scots and Picts banded together to make their attack. This was a revolutionary development as the three different races had never before united. We know little of what happened, but the events must have been disastrous for the Romans. The commander of the coastal defences, an official called the Count of the Saxon Shore, himself was killed. The shock of these attacks was felt as far as Rome and the Count Theodosius was sent with fresh troops in an effort to tighten up the defences of the province. In our area this simply involved the construction of fortlets and signal stations between the main strongpoints. One was built at Corton (near Lowestoft) and another at Stiffkey. There were probably others, as yet undiscovered or destroyed by the sea.

We do not know how long these measures were successful against the barbarians. At any rate, this last period saw a hopeless struggle by the Romans to turn back a tide that was flowing ever more strongly. The raiders were now starting to look for permanent homes instead of just loot. At this time the first *foederati* appear. These were tribesmen recruited from outside the Empire who were brought in to defend Britain in return for grants of land. One tribe, the Alamanni, were brought from the Rhine in about 370 for this purpose, and numbers of Burgundians and Vandals were also imported. Large quantities of Romano-Saxon pottery have been found in East Anglia which indicate the presence of the *foederati* in our region. We can also gather that these newcomers sometimes got out of hand (viz. the remains of thirty-six people in a burned-out house of about AD 400 at Caister-by-Yarmouth) as lawlessness increased. Possibly the Roman garrisons remaining at the Saxon Shore forts were able to prevent the worst excesses of mutinous *foederati*, but in 407–8 a large force of Romans had to be taken to the Continent, and the defence of East Anglia was left to the wild mercenary warriors.

The Romans were in fact able to send an army back to Britain ten years later. This was just a last forlorn hope of keeping Britain as a Roman province and only the south-east could be held, the rest of Britain being too strongly occupied by marauding Picts, Scots and Saxons. Certainly, East Anglia was never re-occupied. Possibly by this time the life style of the inhabitants of the Romano-British townships had disappeared under pressure from the mutinous *foederati*, who were being joined by their kinsmen from over the North Sea. The last Roman soldier finally left Britain in AD 425. By then a tribal Anglo-Saxon society was starting to develop in East Anglia, and the walled Roman towns lay deserted as the period we call the Dark Ages drew on.

3

ANGLO-SAXON EAST ANGLIA

The first settlers

THE story of Anglo-Saxon East Anglia begins long before the last Roman soldier left these islands. In the last chapter we saw how, during the course of the fourth century AD, the vulnerable east coast of Britain came under increasingly fierce attack from fearsome sea-raiders. It was in an effort to defeat these Pictish, Scottish and Saxon pirates that the Count Theodosius re-organized the defences of the Roman province. Among the measures which were taken was the transportation of a Germanic tribe, the Alamanni, to Britain as *foederati* (mercenary auxiliaries) to defend the Romano-British population.

Much of our knowledge of these early settlers comes from the archaeological finds that have been made in our region. Naturally, most of the remains have been discovered at Roman military sites, including Caister-by-Norwich and Burgh Castle, but a surprising amount of pottery has come to light, not in the fortresses, but in the towns nearby. This has led archaeologists to think that there was a large-scale settling of land by Anglo-Saxon tribes with the consent of the local Roman administration. Probably there were two good reasons why the presence of the newcomers was so welcomed. First, the settlers were loosely related to many of the Saxon pirate bands, so that their settlements would be more immune from attack. Second, the presence of numbers of these warriors, prepared to defend their new lands, would have had a deterrent effect on the raiders.

The newcomers who followed the Alamanni to East Anglia were all Germanic in origin, coming from Denmark and north-west Germany. The name 'Anglia' derives from the settlers who came

Opposite Nothing remains above ground, but aerial photography shows the trace of the walls of the Roman 'Saxon shore' fort of Branodunum near Brancaster, Norfolk.

here from 'Angelus', which is the modern area of Angeln in southern Denmark. In addition, people from Swabia also made the journey to these shores; their presence is commemorated in the place name 'Swaffham' – there is a Swaffham in west Norfolk, and another in Cambridgeshire. It is from clues like the origins of village names that scholars have built up a picture of the pattern of this early migration. We can visualize the bands of warriors with their families and livestock crammed into the long, open boats to begin the long row to East Anglia. For, unlike the later Viking ships, the Anglo-Saxon vessels had no sails, and were simply clinker-built rowing boats up to seventy-seven feet long. They were shallow in draught, sitting on the water rather than in the water and consequently the settlers were able to use the rivers to penetrate into the hinterland of East Anglia. Many bands used the rivers which flow into the Wash, and established themselves on the edges of the Fens, in north and west Norfolk, the Breckland area, and also around the site of modern Norwich. So, really, it is more correct to think of the Anglo-Saxon invasion as being like the English colonization of America rather than as a conquest like that of 1066.

As the immigrant bands trickled into East Anglia, the Dark Ages were falling over Europe. The Saxon Shore forts were probably evacuated about AD 407 and, although the Romans were able to send an army from Gaul to Britain ten years later in a last desperate attempt to hold the province, it seems unlikely that the East Anglian forts were ever re-occupied. Resistance to the barbarians was thus left in the hands of the *foederati*. Finally the Romans left, never to return, in 425, and their departure signalled the rise of local tyrants who attempted to keep the raiders at bay. It was with this aim in view that Vortigern of Kent settled new contingents of Anglo-Saxon *foederati* in East Anglia. We know that these men revolted against their employer and

Saxon glassware found at Burgh Castle, Suffolk. Comparison of this kind of ware with finds on the Continent, enables archaeologists to plot migratory patterns of particular tribes.

Opposite Pagan Vikings slay the Christian King Edmund in 'grim rollicking style'—from a painting by H. Payne. Edmund died in 870, probably at Hellesdon near Norwich. The best known of English martyr-saints, Bury St Edmunds is named after him.

seized power for themselves. This obviously must have had the effect of encouraging further groups of their kinsmen to settle here. In fact, a great deal of archaeological work is being carried on at the present time to distinguish all the different tribes and groups. By comparing East Anglian and Continental remains it has been possible to link some settlers with the North Frisian islands and others with Schleswig-Holstein.

Between 500 and 550, there occurred some extremely important events in the history of East Anglia. Generally, this period was characterized by the arrival of fresh invaders who brought East Anglia under the control of a single political dynasty who founded a kingdom.

We have seen how the early settlers used the local rivers to penetrate inland, descending mostly on the more northerly part of our region. Later, as their numbers grew, they still remained in the same area, clustering along the Icknield Way and with access to the east Fenland waterways. The next wave of invaders came not here but to the untouched (by Anglo-Saxons) country of the Suffolk coast, the Sandlings. Today this area has been designated as being of outstanding natural beauty, and many parts are still heavily wooded, as they must have been when the boats of the newcomers first pulled up the rivers to seek the good farming land. Ipswich was first settled in this period, but it was the nearby Deben that attracted the heaviest concentration of settlers. The royal seat was at Rendlesham (probably hidden under the modern national forest) while the royal cemetery has been discovered at Sutton Hoo, overlooking the river. This new wave of invaders were of different origin from the people already in East Anglia. They had come to the

Viking 'sea steeds' like these ships made the North Sea a highway for raiders, rather than a defence for their victims. One Viking fleet was beaten by Alfred the Great in 884, at the confluence of the Stour and Orwell.

Sandlings from the northern part of Jutland in Denmark, but they were not Jutes. Their true homeland was the Scania and Halland provinces of Sweden, and they had settled briefly in Denmark before moving on again.

One point must be mentioned about the way in which all the Anglo-Saxons made the voyage to Britain. It is quite incorrect to think of them simply rowing straight across the North Sea. They actually coasted to Belgium, hugging the shores of Europe in their frail craft, before turning and crossing to Kent. From here, they rowed northwards across the Thames estuary to halt finally in the unoccupied but fertile region of south-east Suffolk.

The Wuffingas

Once settled in their new home, the Sandlings people quickly began to expand and dominate all of East Anglia. The leader of the tribe was an adventurous Swedish warrior-prince called Wehha. It was Wehha's son Wuffa who gave his name to the royal dynasty (the Wuffingas). This indicates that the kingdom was probably not fully consolidated until after Wehha's death.

We are able to plot the course of the rise of the kingdom with such certainty because of a vital difference between the culture of the Sandlings folk and that of the earlier settlers. While the latter cremated their dead, the Sandlings dead were interred. Scientific dating of the contents of Anglo-Saxon cemeteries tells us whether the Sandlings culture had extended into a certain area by a certain date, and thus gives a hint as to the military expansion of Wehha's people.

Earlier we talked of the ruggedness of the country, especially the almost impenetrable belt of dense forest covering High Suffolk, which separated the older settlements from the Sandlings. How, one might ask, could one group establish sovereignty over such a vast area when communications were so difficult? The answer lies in an entirely new factor – sea power. It was the use of ships that enabled the settlers of this remote corner of East Anglia to dominate the old towns that since the earliest times had been the centres of government of the native tribes. It is possible to speculate on how the new arrivals set off to conquer the region, perhaps under the leadership of Wuffa himself. Rowing north from the Deben, Wuffa would have entered each river estuary in turn, exploring the new land and seeking out signs of human habitation. In the Alde, he would have found a settlement at Snape, but would probably not have been able to push much further up the shallow stream. Similarly on the Waveney, he would have seen a desolate sandy island where modern Yarmouth stands, but the ruins of the Roman town of Caister stood on the north bank, and Burgh Castle on the south. Bungay was inhabited, and at the junction of the Yare and the Wensum, where Norwich now stands, the explorers would have found a rash of new settlements. After prowling round the north Norfolk coast, which has no rivers of any size, Wuffa would next have entered each of the Fenland rivers that drain into the Wash. Here he would have found many communities, most of them newly-established, but would not have been able to get much farther south than Cambridge, where the shallowness of the streams would have made further exploration impossible.

The Heptarchy

The kingdom was probably made loyal to the Wuffing dynasty by the frequent visits of sea-borne warriors bearing the trappings of royalty and demanding homage. All this is speculation, of course, but it seems to be the natural way in which the far-flung communities of East Anglia were welded into a unit. But even as this kingdom was emerging, the same pattern was being repeated over all England. Eventually, by the middle of the sixth century, there were seven separate Anglo-Saxon kingdoms: East Anglia, Essex, Sussex, Kent, Wessex, Mercia, and Northumbria.

Essex started to develop as a quite separate kingdom from East Anglia. The early settlers here were Saxons rather than the Angles – who occupied Norfolk – and had much in common with the other Saxon kingdoms, Wessex and Sussex. Too much should not be made of the difference, as the whole area from the Thames to the Wash forms one cultural unit. What is important is that Wehha's people, coming from the south, would have found Essex occupied by a powerful, well-established race, and the Sandlings would have been the first empty

land they came to. This also explains why expansion took place to the north, rather than the south and why the Stour was the boundary between the two kingdoms.

The relations between the seven kingdoms (known collectively as the Heptarchy) were generally hostile and often flared into open war. Each kingdom in turn tried to obtain sovereignty over the others, each king having pretensions to the title 'Bretwalda' or 'ruler of Britain'. In the early seventh century, the 'Bretwalda' was King Aethelbert of Kent. On his death, Raedwald of East Anglia managed to impose his overlordship on the other kingdoms for a short time. Raedwald's major victory was over Northumbria, and he was able to place a puppet king, Edwin, on the Northumbrian throne. Such was the transitory state of domination between the kingdoms that Edwin in turn was able to exercise control over most of southern England by 628. At this time, however, the major military threat to East Anglia came from King Penda of Mercia. The problems that beset East Anglia can be largely attributed to the lack of a strong leader. Raedwald, the greatest East Anglian king, was succeeded by his son Eorpwald, who quickly fell victim to a usurper, being murdered in the process. This murderer was himself deposed by Sigeberht, another son of Raedwald, who abdicated in order to enter a monastery. He was replaced by his kinsman, Ecgric, but both were killed in the fighting against Mercia. The next king was Anna, a nephew of Raedwald, who reigned from 636–655, the last of the fighting kings of East Anglia.

The visitor to the region can see a number of military sites associated with the wars of the seventh century. Mention has already been made of the Icknield Way's immense strategic value. Running up from the south, it constituted the only possible invasion route into East Anglia, lying as it does between dense forest and impassable fen. It was here that the fighting took place, and the East Anglian army's defences can still clearly be seen. For in an effort to stop the invading Mercians the East Anglians raised four lines of massive earthworks right across the Icknield Way.

The first, and most southerly, lies about five miles east of Royston, and is known as the Brand or Heydon Ditch. One end rests on the pond at Melbourn, the other on the woods at Heydon. It lies right across the present A505 out of Royston, about half a mile from the village of Bridgefoot. The next work, the Pampisford Ditch, is smaller, running from Pampisford (again on the A505) in a south-

Persuaded to leave his cell and lead an army against Penda, King of Mercia, Sigebert, the king-monk declined to arm himself other than with a wooden staff. He was killed *c.* AD 633–7.

easterly direction for two miles. Two batches of headless skeletons have been found near the Heydon dyke, but apart from these there is very little of interest here, especially to the casual visitor, as only sections of the old rampart still remain. The next defence, the Fleam Dyke, is much longer and much better preserved. It runs from Balsham to Fen Ditton (the name Fen Ditton means 'the fen ditch-end') and crosses the A11 at a point two miles north of Worsted Lodge. Look out for it about 800 yards

past the cross-roads where the Fulbourne–Balsham road meets the A11. There is a gap in the rampart at Fulbourne, and the dyke cannot be seen again until it rises on the north side of the A45 Cambridge–Newmarket road just outside the last buildings of Cambridge, and from here it runs to Fen Ditton. Unfortunately, there is so much major road reconstruction going on here at the moment that it is impossible to give detailed directions of how best to see it. Indeed, part of the dyke may be obliterated altogether.

The last dyke is easily the most impressive, and is also the easiest to find. It is fully seven miles long, running from Stretchworth across Newmarket

Heath to the fen at Reach. To find it, continue on along the A45 from the Fleam Dyke until, after another ten miles, you come to the huge modern roundabout where the A11 and A45 join. Stop about fifty yards up on the Newmarket side of the round-about and look over the thick hedge that borders the left-hand side of the road. The view is remark-able, for there, almost invisible to the casual passing motorist, lies the last line of defence of the Anglo-Saxon kingdom of East Anglia: a gigantic earthen rampart, eighteen feet high, twelve feet thick at the top, and with a ditch in front so that the length of wall from the bottom of the ditch to the top of the rampart is almost a hundred feet. The chalky soil has kept its shape remarkably well, and a short walk along the ditch reveals just how formidable this defence was, for in most places the slope can only be scaled by scrambling up it on all fours. Any Mercian attacker would have made an easy target for an East Anglian spear if there was an attempt to storm the dyke in the face of a spirited defence. This last work is known as the 'Devil's Dyke', probably because later Norman invaders found it impossible to believe that human hands were responsible for such a large-scale construction.

Today, if one plots the course of these defences on a map, they seem pointless because each end hangs 'in the air'. But if one recalls that in Saxon times the fens were undrained and the forest came

The remains of Burgh Castle stare out across Breydon Water today. The west wall has collapsed, but the deserted castle would have frowned across the water at the Wuffinga princes hundreds of years ago as they probed the Waveney.

Opposite above The Devil's Dyke is the greatest earthwork in the region. Here it is crossing Newmarket Heath where it was the scene of many bloody encounters between the East Anglians and the Mercians. Most probably the Dyke fell as a defence through a combination of assault and treachery.

Opposite below Another view of the Devil's Dyke, which runs from Stretchworth to Reach. Although they have no conclusive proof authorities suggest the Dyke pre-dates the Romans. It is certain that it was used by the Anglo-Saxon kingdom of East Anglia as its last line of defence.

Above The Fleam Dyke at Mutlow Hill. This defensive work runs across the Icknield Way. Its course can be seen from the air although at ground level little remains after centuries of ploughing and modern construction works have transformed the site.

right to the eastern edge of the chalky ridge, the genius of the builders can be fully appreciated. The gap in the Fleam Dyke at Fulbourne and Wilbraham Fen can probably be explained by the fact that nature alone provided sufficient defence here in the form of an impenetrable morass.

Anna, the last opponent of the Mercians, made his base midway behind the Devil's Dyke at St Mildred's Wells near Exning (two miles north of Newmarket on the B1103). From here he could send reinforcements south to the forward lines of defence, and keep open communications with his 'North Folk' and his 'South Folk'. A large Anglo-Saxon cemetery has been excavated near Exning, and the injuries on a number of the skeletons bear witness to the slaughter that must have occurred. Ultimately, Penda was able to take the defences. How he did so we do not know. The *Anglo-Saxon Chronicle*, which is a contemporary history of these times, does tell us that military means were not enough, and that Penda had to resort to intrigue. Anna was killed in the fighting, and was succeeded by his brother Aethelhere who became little more than a vassal of Penda. Both kings were killed the very next year at the battle of the Winwaed, which was fought against the Northumbrians at an unknown site somewhere in Yorkshire.

Sutton Hoo

It seems likely, then, that the decline of the East Anglian kingdom was intimately linked with the loss of control of the Icknield Way. Possibly, too, changing patterns of sea power were also a factor. There is left one magnificent remnant of the kingdom in its heyday – the Sutton Hoo treasure.

In 1939, a team of archaeologists investigated a series of barrows at Sutton Hoo, overlooking the river Deben near Woodbridge. These barrows were extremely prominent, although a nineteenth-century farmer had planted a grove of trees between them and the river. When the largest mound – about twelve feet high and a hundred feet long – was excavated, the archaeologists realized that they had made one of the most important finds of British archaeology: the discovery of no less than the royal cemetery of the kings of East Anglia. In the large barrow were the remains of a ship large enough to take thirty-eight oarsmen, which had been dragged into a deep trench and buried so as to form the mound which would have been visible for miles from the river. In a gabled cabin amidships lay an

incredible amount of treasure. There were no less than forty-one objects of pure gold of the utmost beauty: a helmet, shield and coat of mail; a huge standard of authority; bronze and silver dishes and bowls from as far afield as Byzantium. All this treasure is now in the British Museum.

One problem seemed to be that there was no body in the ship. Two theories have been put forward to explain the absence of a corpse. The first is that the burial ship contains the treasure of some king whose body rests in an unknown place – possibly a king who died in battle and was never buried. The second theory is that Sutton Hoo was the work of some pagan followers of a Christian king, who buried the king's worldly goods in case Christianity was mistaken, and men did in fact need their possessions in the afterlife. A hoard of coins was found in the ship, and these have been dated to between AD 650 and 670. The barrow therefore may be a cenotaph to Anna, the Christian king who died in 655 and whose body lies in the monastery at Blythburgh, Suffolk. Alternatively, it may be the treasure of Aethelhere who was killed in battle in Yorkshire in the same year. Recently (Christmas 1972) the coins have been putatively redated to an earlier period and, if this is correct, the Sutton Hoo treasure may be that of no less a person than great Raedwald himself. One thing is clear. The kings of East Anglia must have been fabulously wealthy to own such goods, and though we tend to think of the Anglo-Saxons as savages in comparison with the Romans, it is certain that they did have a culture that was magnificent in its own right.

To find Sutton Hoo, take the B1438 turning off the A12, and follow it through the main street of Woodbridge to Melton. Then take the B1083 to Sutton, over the river Deben. Turn right and walk down the river bank for a few hundred yards and there, directly ahead on the gently rising ground, lies the last resting place of the men who ruled East Anglia thirteen hundred years ago.

After the collapse of the Icknield Way defences, the kingdom of East Anglia sinks into obscurity. It came under the control of various of the other kingdoms of the Heptarchy, and the Wuffing dynasty came to an end in about 740, two centuries after Wuffa's father had first claimed the land for himself. In 794 a king of East Anglia called Aethelbert was put to death by Offa of Mercia at Sutton Walls near Hereford; but this is one of the few facts that we do know about this period. Even the nominal independence of the kingdom was ended in 823 by Egbert, king of Wessex, who granted an

alliance to the declining kingdom in return for what amounted to total control over it.

The history of the other part of our area, Essex, kingdom of the East Saxons, can be easily told. Both Essex and Sussex were subjugated by Mercia very early in the Anglo-Saxon period. Essex had conquered Middlesex by AD 600 but Aethelbert of Kent drastically checked East Saxon expansion when he captured London, their capital. When Aethelbert died, and East Anglia was reaching its apogee under

The Sutton Hoo helmet. There is no doubt the helmet was worn in battle, over a thousand years ago, by a former ruler of East Anglia but who he was is not yet known.

Sword found at Sutton Hoo. In that age when wars were a regular part of life the martial virtues were of supreme importance. A leader's sword would follow him into the grave, in case he had need of it in after life.

Below The beauty and pains-taking workmanship of this shield boss from the Sutton Hoo treasure are evidence of the high state of culture of the early Anglo-Saxons.

Raedwald, Penda of Mercia swooped down on Essex. After this Essex appears only as a vassal or satellite of some greater power. Essex in fact was the smallest and least significant of the kingdoms of the Heptarchy.

The Vikings

In 793, a new menace from over the North Sea appeared – the Vikings. That year the Viking raiders first ventured out of their Scandinavian homelands to burn and pillage in all the countries of Western Europe. England received her first foretaste of the future when the monastery at Lindisfarne was sacked. The first recorded appearance of the Vikings off East Anglia was in 838, and we do know that they returned in 841. These were just sporadic raids for

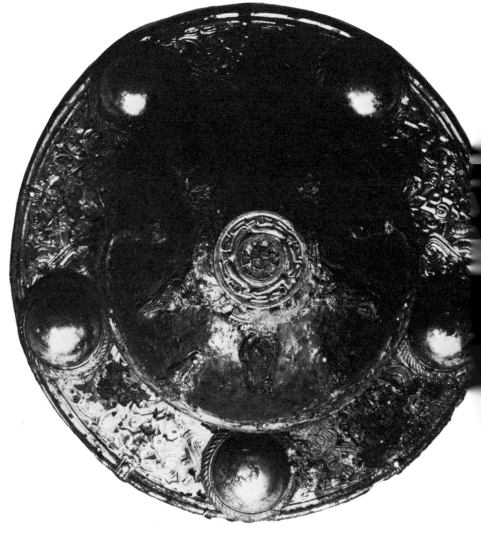

loot; the Viking dragon-ships (equipped with sails as well as oars) vanished as quickly and unpredictably as they appeared. Something rather different happened in 865. This time it was no mere raiding party but a large army that landed in East Anglia, and announced its intention of going into winter quarters. The Viking army had been in France under its leaders Ivar the Boneless and Halfdene. Bought off by Charles the Good, it sought new lands to plunder and descended on Britain's east coast. The kingdom of East Anglia found itself quite unable to resist this horde, and made peace. Throughout the winter the Vikings stayed in Suffolk until, with the coming of spring 866, they prepared to move on. As part of the terms which they had imposed on the East Anglians, the Vikings were to be equipped with horses at East Anglian expense, not because the Vikings were cavalrymen by nature but because horses would give them the mobility to sweep far inland in search of loot, and make it easier to avoid superior local forces if the need arose. Attacking Northumbria first, the Vikings took York in November 866. The next year Mercia was so badly beaten that she was compelled to submit to an ignominious treaty. Thus in three short years three Anglo-Saxon kingdoms had been totally overthrown by the 'Great Army'.

In the autumn of 869, the Vikings returned to East Anglia to spend the winter. They made their headquarters at Thetford on the Icknield Way, and some traces of their stay have been discovered there since the Second World War. Earthworks, consisting of a rampart and a ditch forty feet wide have been found running from the Red Castle via the St Mary's Estate to the Nun's Bridges over the Thet and the Little Ouse. Neither the mound of the Red Castle nor the mound called Castle hill (which is the largest motte, or castle mound, in England) belong to this age; both are later Norman works. We do know a few facts about that winter, but there is much that still remains a mystery. It is certain that the Vikings rode out of Thetford to ravage the East Anglian monasteries at Ramsey, Ely, Soham and Thorney; and it is possible that the East Anglians fought back, because there are records of conflicts. At Framlingham for instance, a Saxon fortress stood on the site of the medieval castle whose ruins dominate the town today, and in 869–70 an East Anglian king called Edward was besieged there by the Vikings. This Edward is perhaps a misspelling of Edmund, for we do know that a king of East Anglia called Edmund was killed by the Vikings that same winter. Edmund was tied to a tree and his body was shot full of arrows at a place called 'Haegelsdun', which is taken to be modern Hellesdon on the outskirts of Norwich. It is probable that Norwich was burned by raiders coming by boat up the Yare, and that Edmund tried to stop them, for even then Norwich was an important settlement. If so, Edmund's terrible fate served as a grim warning to anyone else disposed to oppose the invaders. Edmund was canonized and he is commemorated by the name Bury St Edmunds. There is a very early tradition that says that he was in fact buried in the royal cemetery at Sutton. It may be that one day archaeologists will open one of the other barrows on that ridge overlooking the Deben and find his remains. It would be a discovery of primary ecclesiastical as well as archaeological importance.

Alfred the Great

When spring came and the new grass was able to supply the Viking horses with their forage, the 'Great Army' moved once again. This time their opponent was to be a kingdom which alone stood between them and the mastery of all southern England – Wessex. The young king of Wessex was Alfred the Great, known to every schoolboy because of the legend of the burnt cakes. After four years of constant fighting, the Viking leaders began to quarrel. It seemed to some that Wessex would never be taken and so, in despair, half of the 'Great Army' followed their leaders to the Tyne in search of easier loot. The remainder, under a chief called Guthrum, returned to Cambridge.

Guthrum still had hopes of conquering Wessex, and in 876 he planned a two-pronged attack on Alfred. While a Viking army from Ireland landed at Poole, Guthrum was to march overland and take Alfred in the rear. At first successful, Guthrum was badly defeated at Ethandun in 878, and forced to make peace. The Vikings agreed to live in peace with Wessex, and in return Alfred accepted that East Anglia was Viking territory. So in 880 Guthrum settled in East Anglia and shared out the land that had been won. At Cambridge, Huntingdon and Bedford independent boroughs (from 'burh' meaning 'fortified place') were set up, each with its own army and ruled by a 'jarl'. Guthrum himself kept a large part of central East Anglia, including the modern towns of Ipswich, Colchester, Norwich and Thetford. Hadleigh, in Suffolk, was the site of Guthrum's own settlement.

In 884, a mere four years later, another Viking

army returning from the Continent landed in Kent, which was part of Alfred's Wessex. Guthrum, seeing a new opportunity of taking Wessex, prepared to join the newcomers. Before the two forces could unite, Alfred won a splendid victory over the invaders at Rochester, throwing them right out of Kent. The remnants of the Viking force took to their ships in an attempt to reach their ally Guthrum at his home in Hadleigh, which stands on the Brett, a tributary of the Stour. Since the very beginning of the Viking raids, it had been this kind of mobility that had made the raiders such formidable opponents. Not only could they move freely, but they could also choose the spot they wished to attack, and retreat to the sea if anything went wrong. Alfred, however, had built up a fleet of his own, developed with the idea of harrying the Vikings on the water. After defeating the Vikings on the land, Alfred sent his fleet in hot pursuit of the Viking ships. It was off the mouth of the Stour, on the stretch of water directly in front of HMS *Ganges*, the naval training barracks, that Alfred's fleet caught up with the Vikings. Here, where the large merchant ships lie at anchor today, sixteen Viking vessels were taken and burnt, and their crews unceremoniously drowned. The spit of land covered by the barracks is still known as 'Bloody Point'. Alfred's fleet did not go unscathed, for Guthrum's long-ships intercepted it on its return to Kent and defeated it. But the damage to the Vikings had been done, and the events of 884 must be counted as one of the earliest English sea victories.

Alfred and Guthrum were still clashing in a series of skirmishes across southern Essex. The sites of these are unknown, but the campaign culminated in the capture of London by Alfred. Peace was made again between the two leaders. Alfred agreed that the Viking territory, called the Danelaw, should be marked by the Thames, the Lea as far as Bedford, then up the Ouse. Thus it comprised East Anglia, with parts of Huntingdonshire, Hertfordshire and Bedfordshire. Danes also controlled the East Midlands and the land north of the Humber. So, to sum up the situation in 886: Alfred was king over all southern England as defined by a line from the Thames north to Huntingdon, then north-west across England to the mouth of the Mersey, following the old Roman Watling Street, which is more or less the present A5. The Danelaw should not be thought of as a unified kingdom but as a number of loosely-connected settlements under various warrior chiefs. Guthrum, the leading warrior, never had the opportunity to break this latest agreement – he died peacefully at Hadleigh in 890.

Fighting broke out again in 892, when England was once again invaded. In 879, some veterans of the 'Great Army' had gone raiding in Gaul until, faced by mounting opposition there, they returned across the Channel. Under a leader called Haestern, 'a lusty and terrifying old warrior', eighty shiploads of them landed in Kent. Alfred, after taking hostages from the East Anglian Danes to ensure their good behaviour, attempted to negotiate with Haestern. While terms were being talked, Alfred was double-crossed by the Vikings. Haestern sent his ships to Benfleet in Essex and started a long, circuitous raid, intending to ravage the Home Counties, cross the Thames above London and rejoin the ships at Benfleet. Alfred's son, Edward, set off in hot pursuit. He beat the Vikings at Farham but was unable to stop them reaching their ships at Benfleet. The Vikings were confident, however, and offered battle. Pausing only long enough to collect reinforcements, Edward plunged in to the attack.

The battle of Benfleet is extremely unusual in that the Vikings fought from behind fortifications. Haestern had had his ships dragged on to the bank of the stream so as to be safe from foul weather and guarded more easily. Round the beach a rampart had been constructed to prevent attack from the landward side. The remains of these defences today are a series of irregular elevations around the church and by the Beam Fleet. Edward stormed the rampart and won a great victory. Few details are known of the fighting, although the *Anglo-Saxon Chronicle* does say that Haestern's ships were either burnt or carried off in triumph to London. This is borne out by archaeological evidence. When the railway bridge that spans the stream was being constructed, remains of a number of charred ships and human skeletons were found in the mud.

After this defeat, Haestern retreated to Shoeburyness in Essex, where another fortified camp was built. Little remains of this camp today except a few fragments of wall. Sea erosion has eaten most of the defences away, and those that are left are on Ministry of Defence property. This camp, we know from a survey of 1879, was massive. It was open to the sea, and was 1,900 feet long and 750 feet broad, defended by a single earth wall and a huge ditch. The Wessex men prudently decided not to risk attacking it. The camp was not in use for very long because the Vikings were reinforced and went on the offensive again. Taking the ships that had escaped the Benfleet disaster, Haestern swept down the Thames and deep into the heart of England by following the Lea to Hertford. As this river was the boundary between Wessex and the Danelaw, Haestern thought himself safe. For by travelling on the Lea, he was not invading Wessex as such; and while he would be able to raid across the frontier, he could also seek refuge in the Danelaw. At this point Alfred played a master-stroke. Once the Viking ships were upstream, he constructed two fortresses, one on each side of the river, and stretched a great boom across the Lea between them. With the Viking ships trapped, the resulting battle and English victory meant that Haestern had to retreat overland into East Anglia. This time Haestern made his camp on Mersea Island, Essex, from where he made his last attack on Wessex. He attacked directly overland, was caught near Bullington, and had his army scattered to the four winds, never again to pose a threat to Wessex.

King Edward of Wessex

Alfred the Great died in 899, leaving two claimants to the throne of Wessex: Edward ('the Elder') his son, and Aethelwold, his brother. The latter made his claim with the help of the Danes. The Danes of East Anglia accepted him as king of Wessex, and in 903 he led their army on a raid into Mercia. Edward replied in 906 by ravaging the country between the Ouse and the Cambridgeshire Dykes. The Danish army came hastening up, only to find that Edward and his army had gone home. The laggardly Kentish contingent allowed themselves to be caught, and were heavily defeated in the ensuing battle. What was important from Edward's point of view was that both Aethelwold and Eorhic, the Danish ruler of East Anglia, were slain in the fighting. With the cause of war thus removed, an uneasy peace reigned over England.

It was obvious to Edward, as it had been to his father, that the only sure way of putting an end to the constant raiding was nothing less than the reconquest of the Danelaw. In 910, the Danes once again raided Mercia, only to be thrown back by Edward and his sister, Queen Aethelflaeda of the Mercians. After campaigning in the north, Edward began the final war against the Danes of East Anglia in 913. The character of these last campaigns was changed by Edward's construction of a chain of fortresses which formed a barrier against the Danish bases. The siting of most of these 'burhs' was in river valleys as their main object was to hamper Viking mobility by denying them the free use of the

water for transport. They also served the purpose of always being a threat to the Danish rear if bypassed, as well as providing jumping-off points for English forays. Edward made them so strong that they could not easily be taken, yet so dangerous that the Danes would not dare leave them uninvested. The fortresses were not forts in the Roman sense, as at Bradwell or Burgh Castle, nor were they like medieval castles, rather they were fortified settlements protected by earthen ramparts and ditches. Consequently, the remains enclose vast areas.

In 913, Edward improved and strengthened the two fortresses on the Lea at Hertford where Haestern had been defeated eighteen years before. Next, a 'burh' was raised at Witham in Essex followed, a year later, by an advance to Buckingham and the building of earthworks there. In 915, Bedford was taken and fortified, while 916 saw the building of defences at Towcester (on Watling Street), at Wigingamere (not yet discovered), and at Maldon in Essex.

These fortresses were put to the test in 917 when the Danes rose in a general war and attempted to break out over the frontiers of the Danelaw. Towcester, which had stone walls of Roman origin, repulsed the attack easily, as did Bedford. Here the Danes were pursued by Edward himself when they fell back, first to Willington on the Ouse, where Edward chased them out of their own earthworks. They stood again at Tempsford, on the modern A1, but were beaten again by Edward and the Danish king was among the dead.

In the south of our region, the Danes were vainly trying to take Maldon. Not only did this fortress on the Blackwater hold out, but the Danes also lost Colchester. The *Anglo-Saxon Chronicle* tells us that Colchester was 'repaired', and the use of this word, rather than the more usual term 'wrought', indicates that the old Roman walls were utilized. Wigingamere was also assaulted this year but, like all of the English works, it held out.

Next year, 918, saw the culmination of Edward's campaign. Edward first advanced to Huntingdon, took it, fortified it, and received the submission of the local Danes. Then he marched down to Colchester, which was to be the base for the final advance against the Danes of Norfolk and Suffolk. No sooner did he appear than Essex, Norfolk and Suffolk all surrendered. A few months later, Cambridgeshire's Danes also gave up the struggle. Their position was hopeless: to the north and east lay the sea, to the west lay a ring of fortresses (Huntingdon had been the last bolt on the door), and Edward and his army were advancing from the south. Throughout this last campaign Edward had displayed the highest standards of generalship, but undoubtedly the fortresses were the deciding factor in his victory.

There are some interesting remains in our region that date from Edward's wars. Witham fortress, lying on slightly rising ground by the River Brain, is the finest. Unfortunately civilization has mutilated the site. A railway cutting slashes right across the earthworks, and Witham railway station lies in the very centre of Edward's fortress. What is remarkable about Witham is that there is a second wall within the outer ring, and this in fact is the only known Anglo-Saxon earthwork with a double enclosure. The outer wall encloses some twenty-six acres, while the area bounded by the inner rampart is about nine acres. The shape of the fortress is a regular oval, measuring 1,200 feet by 1,000, and protected by a ditch almost 30 feet wide.

Of Maldon fortress, little remains now. Deep ploughing has rendered the old rampart almost unrecognizable, but the traces that can still be seen lie to the north-west of the present town of Maldon, where Lodge Road runs down towards the Blackwater. From an account written in 1775, we know that something of great archaeological interest has been lost, for this old survey of the place says quite clearly that there were two concentric lines of defence, as at Witham. The question that must be raised is: why are the only two double-ring fortresses located in southern Essex? It is a question to which the answer will probably never be known now.

Witham and Maldon are the only two 'burhs' of Edward's time that can be positioned with any certainty, and their fate at the hands of industrial development has been the fate of so many of Britain's archaeological sites. The fortress of Wigingamere also probably lies in our region, as it was attacked by the East Anglian Danes. The site of Wigingamere remains to be discovered, although some archaeologists, like C. S. Armitage, have identified it with Wicken, a village on the A1123 about ten miles north-east of Cambridge. This fits the pattern of Edward's other fortresses, as it lies on the Cam, and would thus have hindered Viking mobility along this important river route. Armitage argued that the 'mere' in 'Wigingamere' may be a reference to the great stretch of water running south from the Fens in Saxon days. When the area around Wicken was under water, it may have been called 'Wigingamere'.

A similar case is afforded by another undiscovered fortress, 'Cledemuthan'. Edward built this in 918, the year that East Anglia surrendered to him, to hold the Danes in subjugation and thus keep the peace. The word 'muthan' points to a river estuary. 'Clede' may refer to Cley in Norfolk, which was a thriving port before its harbour silted up. A different location for Cledemuthan is suggested by a chronicler called William of Worcester, who says that Edward repaired Burgh Castle, the old Roman fort near Yarmouth. William confuses Burgh with Norwich, so the mystery of Cledemuthan remains. But the problem of the two forts of Wigingamere and Cledemuthan does show how very sketchy in parts our knowledge of the past is still. It does show, too, how there is always the hope that there will be another major archaeological discovery which will enlighten us a little more about these Dark Ages.

The battle of Maldon

For two generations there was peace in east Anglia until, in 981, the Viking raids started again. A number of factors combined to lead to this. One was the stiffening opposition to the raids led by the Danish king Swein and his son Cnut upon the traditional Viking targets on the Continent. There was also a new spirit of resistance to them in the Celtic countries, which made raids there costly and dangerous. The deciding factor was England's inherent lack of good leadership. For in these times a country was usually only as strong as the personality of the king, and the age of the great fighting kings of Wessex was over. The king in 981 was a weak, unloved waverer known to history as Ethelred the Unready.

Ethelred, who had a long, unhappy reign from 978 until 1016, adopted a policy of bribing the Vikings by the payment of huge sums of money, known as the Danegeld. In the days of Ethelred, the raiding Danish army did just what it liked, and the *Anglo-Saxon Chronicle* tells us that the armies of King Swein were never brought to battle because all were afraid to face them. This is perhaps an exaggeration, but it is certainly true that whenever local forces dared to stand against the Danes, the Danes always beat them.

As the last king of East Anglia had been killed at Tempsford, and East Anglia was part of the unified English kingdom, the region was now governed by an official called an 'earldorman'. Earldormen were usually appointed either from the royal family or a major noble family, and they acted as viceroys, having immense power. Aethelstan of East Anglia, for instance, was known as 'Half-King'. The support of the earldormen was vital to any king, for their chief task was to call out and lead the 'fyrd', the local shire levy of troops.

This is the background to the most important military site in East Anglia, the battlefield of Maldon in Essex. In 991, a Danish army of no less than ninety-three shiploads of men descended on East Anglia. Their first target was Ipswich, which they burned to the ground, and then they took their plunder down to Northey Island, which lies in the Blackwater estuary. Maldon seemed to be the next target and Britnoth, earldorman of Essex, quickly assembled the levies and marched to protect it.

The battlefield has not changed in the course of the last 1,000 years, and is readily accessible. Take the A414 from Chelmsford to Maldon, and go straight through the main street. Follow the B1018, Mundon Road, and a mile further on, just after you pass two long blocks of houses, the entrance to South House Farm leads down to the river. Northey Island lies about 200 yards out in the river, and if you follow the edge of the saltings at low tide, the stone causeway that figured so prominently in the battle becomes visible. The casual visitor should take great care – the causeway is covered at high tide, and on either side of it there is deep mud.

The battle took place on 11 August 991. Britnoth, a giant of six feet nine, drew up his men at the end of the causeway. All on foot, shields locked together to form a protective wall, they waited for the low tide and the Viking assault. Before they attempted to storm across the causeway from the island, they sent a messenger who promised that the Vikings would go home without fighting if the Essex men paid them a tribute of silver and gold.

We are lucky in that a long epic poem, *The Battle of Maldon*, which was written soon after the battle, survives. In it, the events of that day are told in a magnificent style. Any visitor to the battlefield of Maldon is strongly recommended to buy a copy of the poem. The most readily available is the volume called *The Earliest English Poems*, translated by Michael Alexander, and published in the Penguin Classics series. Thus armed, the visitor can more easily imagine that bloody day almost one thousand years ago, and hear again Britnoth's reply to the Vikings:

'Hearest 'ou, seaman, what this folk sayeth?
Spears shall be all the tribute they send you,
viper-stained spears and the swords of forebears,
such a haul of harness as shall hardly profit you.

Spokesman for scavengers, go speak this back
again, bear your tribe a bitterer tale:
that there stands 'mid his men not the meanest
    of Earls,
pledged to fight in this land's defence,
the land of Ethelred, my liege lord,
its soil, its folk.'*

The first Viking assault over the causeway was beaten back easily. With the English holding the end, the Norsemen were quite unable to make headway. At this point English victory seemed assured; and then Britnoth made his fatal mistake. Growing overconfident, he drew his army back a little to allow the Danes to cross in greater numbers. Once established, the Viking archers harassed the English to such effect that they were too confused to attack. Meanwhile, hordes of Vikings swarmed across to support the archers. These formed up in a wedge-shaped formation and hurled themselves into the English ranks with hacking swords. Britnoth himself went down, and the heart went out of the English army. Demoralization turned into rout when a warrior called Godric leapt on to Britnoth's horse to escape. Many of the English thought that this was the Earl himself running away, and naturally followed.

Some of the English stayed, though it meant certain death. In Anglo-Saxon times a lord provided food, shelter and protection for his men, his 'hearth-companions', and in return those men would fight to the death in defence of the lord. Some of the most moving verses of the poem about Maldon come when the hearth-companions resolve to die around Britnoth's body. In the words of Brythwold,

'Courage shall grow keener, clearer the will,
the heart fiercer, as our force faileth.
Here our lord lies levelled in the dust,
the man all marred: he shall mourn to the end
who thinks to wend off from this war-play now.
Though I am white with winters I will not away,
for I think to lodge me alongside my dear one,
Lay me down by my lord's right hand.'

Although this was an English defeat, Britnoth deserves a place among England's heroes, although he is almost forgotten today. His massive skeleton, with a piece of wax instead of the head (which the Vikings had cut off), was found at Ely Cathedral in 1769 during repair work.

* This excerpt is taken from the Penguin translation, as is Brythwold's speech.

Ruins of St Mary's Priory, Thetford. Near here the Vikings raised their earthworks and here they first wintered. Thetford stands at the junction of the Icknield Way and the Little Ouse and both Vikings and Normans realized its strategic importance.

The triumph of the Danes

In 992, King Swein himself came to England to lead his plundering armies. For a time the Danegeld bought him off; but in 1002 Ethelred the Unready organized a mass murder of settlers of Danish extraction. Swein's sister was among those killed, and this brought Swein back to England to have his revenge. The Earldorman of East Anglia was one Ulfcytel, whose fighting ability was so respected by the Vikings that they called our region 'Ulfcytel's land'. In 1004, Ulfcytel attacked Swein near Thetford. A contemporary account tells us that 'many fell dead on both sides. There, the flower of the East Anglian army was killed. But if they had been there in full strength, the Danes would never have got back to their ships; they themselves said that they had never met harder fighting in England than Ulfcytel dealt them.' Apparently the battle was closely drawn, and Ulfcytel ordered some 'country folk' to burn the Viking ships, but they disobeyed him. This is a clue as to the sympathy that many of the settlers in the old Danelaw felt for the invaders. The site of the battle has not been discovered; all we know is that it took place somewhere between Ipswich and Thetford. After it East Anglia was so terribly ravaged that even the Danes were forced to go home in 1005 because of the widespread starvation – a result of their looting.

In 1010, with England's resistance gradually disintegrating, Ulfcytel met the Danes in battle again. A Viking army, led by Thorkell the Tall, had been looting the south coast, and had even besieged London. So devastated was this area that Thorkell resolved to go elsewhere by ship, land, and start a new campaign. He landed at Ipswich and took Swein's route of 1004, intending to march up the Roman Colchester–Brancaster road and strike inland towards Cambridge down the Icknield Way, or follow the Roman road up to the Norwich region. At a spot near Thetford, Ulfcytel drew up his men and waited. He chose his ground well, standing at a place where Peddar's Way, the old Roman road, joins the open chalk of the Icknield Way. Whether Thorkell went north or south-west, he would still have to cut his way past Ulfcytel. To find the battlefield today, take the A11 north out of Thetford. After four miles, take the left fork down the minor road off the A11. Two miles further on (about four hundred yards before the point where the minor road joins the B1110) a pond lies on the left-hand side of the road. This is Ringmere Pit, after which the battle is named.

Here, in May 1010, Thorkell went in to the attack. His army was superb. Among it was a force of forty-five shiploads of warriors from Jomsberg, 'Jomsvikings', who were the most disciplined fighters of those days. The Jomsvikings originated from the island of Wallin at the mouth of the Oder, and were a kind of fighting guild, governed by their own rules and statutes of behaviour. Against such men the English were helpless. The East Anglian fyrd gave way almost straight away, but the Cambridgeshire men held on for a while. Then, at the height of the battle, treachery reared its head again. A nobleman of Danish extraction with the fascinating name Thurcytel the Ant-Head, defected from the English ranks, starting a panic among the Cambridgeshire warriors. It was another splendid Viking victory, and East Anglia was at their mercy again. But it had been another hard-fought battle, and the dead lay in heaps around Ringmere pond. An ancient manuscript tells us,

'Hringmara heath
was a bed of death.
Haarfager's heir
dealt slaughter there.'

In the next few months, the conquering Danes sent Thetford and Peterborough up in flames, and held Crowland to ransom. There is a legend that one man escaped the wrath of the Vikings at Balsham by defending himself on the winding stairs of the church tower, where the Vikings could only attack him singly. There must have been numbers of bitter unrecorded skirmishes during these years. Swords, daggers, amulets and shield bosses inscribed with mystic runes, all mixed with a tangle of human and animal bones, were found in 1875 at Hauxton Mill, which is the site of a ford across the Cam. There must be many more similar sites as yet undiscovered.

At length, in 1015, Swein died in England. To the East Anglians, it seemed as if St Edmund himself had answered their prayers, and one ancient chronicler tells us that the holy martyr 'smote Sweyn the tyrant, that he died'. This did not bring an end to England's sufferings, for Swein was succeeded by his son Canute. Canute was accepted as king by those parts of England under Danish domination, and he carried on the fight. In 1016 the unlamented Ethelred the Unready died, and the new king of Wessex was his son, Edmund Ironside. Canute was besieging London, and then travelled by sea first to Ipswich then to the River Crouch, where he confronted Edmund at Ashingdown. It was to be the last battle of the Anglo-Saxon period.

While the ships lay in the river, Canute formed up on the level ground between the swamps of the Crouch and Ashingdown Hill. The English came charging down the hill, and for once the Danes wavered. Then, once again, it was treachery or stupidity that lost the day. Earl Edric and his men fled with a portion of the English army, and the rest were defeated. Ulfcytel died there, as did most of the leading English nobles. Canute pursued Edmund into Gloucestershire, and concluded with him an agreement that the Danes should have the territory which they had won, and this included East Anglia.

Edmund died about eighteen months later, and the West Saxons accepted Canute as their king. As Canute was also the king of Denmark, 1017 marks the amalgamation of the two kingdoms, the end of the Viking raids, and the ultimate victory of the Danes. Thorkell the Tall, victor of Ringmere, became the new Earldorman of East Anglia in place of the dead Ulfcytel. Peace descended on our region for fifty years, and it is possible that even today England might have been part of a Scandinavian Empire, were it not for the arrival of a new group of conquerors in 1066 – the Normans.

4

THE MIDDLE AGES

The Norman conquest

1066 is probably the best known date in all English history. It is one of the few true watersheds by which we split our past into different ages; for it represents the introduction of a new ruling class, and the beginning of feudal society. The Normans who followed Duke William to England were the descendants of Vikings who had been given the region around Rouen by Charles the Simple in about 911. This Duchy, Normandy, was a powerful, aggressive state which had expanded its frontiers considerably by the eleventh century. Its society was a military society which is called feudalism. Feudalism essentially involves each social class having land tenure from its immediate superior in return for homage and military service. The king was the ultimate lord, granting vast estates to the leading noblemen, and expecting from them the same loyalty and service that they themselves demanded from their tenants. This system had developed in Western Europe during the eighth century, after the break-up of Charlemagne's empire, when there was no central authority to prevent the incursions of Moors and Vikings. The power of the state became decentralized and diffused among the barons, who had a degree of autonomy that would be quite unthinkable in a modern state.

These facts about the nature of medieval society underlie the military history of the Middle Ages. For feudalism gave rise to the Norman military innovation – the privately-owned castle. While the private castle appeared on the Continent in the ninth century, it was unknown in England until after the Conquest. The 'burhs', or 'fortified places', of Edward the Elder were not the same. They were large settlements, built by royal authority, designed to shelter and protect the whole community. The Norman castle was the private residence of one man and his household, a symbol of his power and a defence against his neighbours. Also, many of the leading nobles were almost as powerful as the king, and thus we see over the whole of the Middle Ages a struggle to effect the gradual strengthening of the Crown and the curtailment of the power of the barons.

On 14 October 1066, the Normans defeated the English at the battle of Hastings. It was, effectively, the death blow of the English cause. Their king, Harold, had been killed and they offered no resistance as the invaders marched around London. The left wing of the Norman army raided up the Icknield Way as far as Cambridge before William was crowned king on Christmas Day, 1066. In three short months the Normans had taken their new kingdom, overcome the token resistance of the English and established a new dynasty.

Norman castles

Throughout 1067 the new governors consolidated their hold. Most of the Norman knights had followed William in return for grants of land in England. Cambridge was part of the earldom of Earl Walthof, who was won to the Conqueror's cause by promises of a marriage alliance with William's family. Norfolk and Suffolk, once the earldom of King Harold himself, had been held by one of his brothers at the time of the Conquest. He was replaced by a Norman, Ralph de Guader, who settled at Norwich. Meanwhile, all over East Anglia the lesser nobles were consolidating their hold on their estates. We can imagine them choosing the sites of their new castles, then rounding up the English country folk to slave in gangs on the symbols of their own domination.

Most of these early castles were not stone but quick, cheap structures called motte and baileys. They consisted of a large earth mound, the motte, surrounded at the base by a ditch, and usually with a rampart or palisade around the summit. The lord lived in a wooden tower on top of this motte. At the foot of the mound there was a large enclosure defended by earth rampart and ditch. The ditch was continuous with that of the motte, so that the ditches resembled an overbalanced figure eight. The castle remains which survive to this day usually represent the work of generations of castle builders, each rebuilding, extending and improving the earlier work; so that there are few castles that can be dated to a single period. Despite this, there are a number of interesting remains of the motte and bailey castle in our region.

At Thetford is the largest motte in England. In an age when the average mound was between twenty and thirty feet, Thetford towers a full hundred feet. Ely was a typical motte and bailey, the remains of which can be seen on the side of the A142, just before the cathedral. A degree of improvization can be seen at the old Roman fort at Burgh Castle. There the Normans built a motte in the south-west corner of the fort wall, and erected a U-shaped ditch in front of it. At Castle Acre in Norfolk there is a second small bailey which guards the approaches to the motte, while a further enclosure to the south-west would have contained the village which grew up in the shelter of the castle. A similar arrangement can also be seen at Pleshey.

It was not only the nobles who were building castles during the early Norman period. The Conqueror himself is responsible for some of the remains in our region. In 1068, two of the English northern earls, Edwin and Morcar, raised a rebellion in Yorkshire. William took the field in person to put them down, and on his return journey to London he established a chain of castles designed to safeguard communications with the north. Lincoln and Huntingdon date from this scheme, but the castle that is of particular interest to us is Cambridge. It was built on the north bank of the river, near the county gaol, in an old Roman enclosure. No buildings remain on it today as it was destroyed during the Civil War by Oliver Cromwell, who used it as an earthwork to protect Cambridge from a royalist advance from Huntingdon. There is still a substantial mound which makes an interesting viewpoint.

Resistance to the Conqueror

Trouble threatened William the following year when King Sweyn of Denmark gathered an invasion force to press his claim to the English throne, which was based on his relationship with Cnut (or Canute, as he is more popularly known). Some of the Danish landing parties were repulsed in Kent, but made further landings at Ipswich after sailing up the Orwell, that traditional invasion route of the Norsemen. These Danes were not the fearsome warriors of yesteryear, and were defeated easily by the local levies at some unknown site, probably near Nacton. The Danes withdrew, but struck at Norwich, where Ralph de Guader beat them. There was one consequence of Sweyn's raid. William realized that he needed a castle of his own in East Anglia to act as a centre of resistance against any further invasion attempts. The result was Colchester Castle – the finest Norman keep in Britain. This was no earth and timber structure, but a mighty stone work designed to withstand any assault.

We do not know the actual date when the construction started. Colchester, in fact, was burned in 1071 by Danish raiders, and the work may not have been under way by then; but it is true to say that it was Sweyn's raid of 1069 that first showed the need for a royal fortress in East Anglia. The castle today stands in a park in the main street of Colchester. The foundations were already there, for the keep stands on the massive marble of the old Roman Temple of Claudius, which had withstood the wrath of the Iceni one thousand years before. The huge rectangular keep was originally one storey high, surmounted by ramparts and battlements. At a later date, another storey was added, and there were also turrets reaching above the level of the main walls. These were destroyed in 1648 after the bitter fighting during the Royalist revolt. The Great Hall was roofed over in 1932, and the town museum is now housed there. Measuring 152 feet by 111 feet, the keep is a splendid reminder of Colchester's link with William the Conqueror.

But to return to Sweyn's raiders. After their defeat at the hands of Ralph de Guader, they sailed north to the Humber and landed again. This was the area that had seen a revolt the previous year, and the Danes received such a warm welcome from disaffected English groups that they were able to occupy York. When William came storming up from the south, the Anglo-Danish army made no attempt to face him at York, but tumbled back to the shelter of the Danish fleet in the Humber. William had to turn aside to deal with Mercia, which had flared into open rebellion, and the Danes seized the opportunity to re-occupy York. William won an easy victory at Stafford and came to settle accounts with the Danes at last. He cut a terrible swathe of destruction through Yorkshire, and before he could invest York the Danes came to terms. They agreed to leave on condition that they were allowed to winter around the mouth of the Humber. William granted them these terms, but it was a decision that was to cost East Anglia dear.

That winter, a number of the Danes drifted into the Fenland to await the coming of spring. Once there, they decided not to return home without some loot, and in 1070 they established a camp in the Isle of Ely. The Isle was the base for a figure much distorted by romantic legend: the guerrilla leader known to history as Hereward the Wake. With Earl Osbern, the Danish leader, Hereward developed the idea of sacking the monastery at Peterborough, a fabulously wealthy and important prize. What interested him was that the Danes had ships; so that his forces would not have to attack overland, but could use the waterways of the Fens to achieve complete surprise. That is what happened. The Danish ships, guided by the English rebels who knew the treacherous area so well, crept up the river Nene to catch the monks before they had time to hide any of the priceless treasures which the monastery owned. The great religious house was completely sacked. The abbot rode for help, but by the time he returned at the head of a band of knights the destruction was complete, the Danish ships had left and Hereward had retreated safely to his marshy lair.

The sack of Peterborough must have come as a blow to William, who had thought his realm finally free from revolt. Worse was to come next year, however, when the Earls Edwin and Morcar raised the countryside once again. This rebellion was a minor affair which fizzled out when Edwin was murdered. The problem which beset William was that Morcar, together with a powerful East Anglian landowner called Siward Born, had sought shelter with Hereward in the Fens. William was thus faced by the potentially dangerous combination of Hereward's ability and the charisma of Morcar, who was of the English royal house and who could act as a figurehead for widespread English resistance to the Normans. Consequently the reduction of Ely was of primary importance, and elaborate plans were made accordingly.

First the seaward exits were cut off when the king's ships penetrated the River Ouse. Then the king set out to take the landward defences. The main route into the Isle of Ely in Norman times was from the south. A causeway ran from Lolworth (on the modern A604), via Longstanton and Willingham,

across the Great Ouse (formerly called the West River) and through Aldreth to Ely. Today, a footpath runs north from Willingham across the fields to the Great Ouse, safely contained by its steep man-made banks. Then it was a track through the marsh, and the Great Ouse was a perplexing obstacle for the military engineers to overcome. The only course open to William was to attempt to build a causeway across the bog, and this is what he did. Large beams and logs were brought up and bound together in the water; underneath them were placed the inflated hides of freshly-flayed sheep to counteract the weight of the advancing men at arms.

The first assault was resoundingly and cunningly defeated when Hereward set the causeway alight. William made a second attempt, and this time broke into the Isle. Hereward escaped, though Morcar and Siward were taken. To ensure that Ely would never rise again, William built a motte and bailey castle at Ely. We also know that another fortress 'Alrehede', was erected for the same purpose. 'Alrehede' is obviously Aldreth, where the assault took place; the difficulty is that there are two different sites which have each been identified with the castle of Aldreth. The first is the huge earthwork (880 feet across) called Belsar's Hill at Willingham, two miles south of Aldreth. This site would have guarded the south end of William's causeway over the Great Ouse. Alternatively, the castle may be identified with the earthwork that lies east of the A10 at Braham Farm, a mile south of Ely. A number of eleventh-century spearheads have been found here. Both places of course may be connected with William's campaign, but it is uncertain which is 'Alrehede'.

Norman revolts against William

The warfare in the Fens marked the last English opposition to the Normans in our area. From now on, attention falls on revolts of the Norman barons against the Crown. In view of what is to come, it might be asked why the king did not strip the barons of their castles. The answer is that until the Crown was rich enough to maintain a stipendiary army and its own garrisons, the baronial castles formed an essential element in the defences of the realm.

The first Norman revolt against William broke out in 1075, and was not serious. It involved our region, however, in the person of Ralph de Guader, Earl of Norfolk. He and Roger, Earl of Hereford,

Castle Acre, Norfolk. Originally a Roman camp guarded the passage of the Peddar's Way. Later William de Warrenne built his castle with three baileys one of which contains the village.

planned to overthrow the king, who was absent in Normandy, and divide the realm between them. In the absence of William, military affairs were in the hands of an official called the Justiciar. At this time, the Justiciar was another East Anglian landowner, William de Warrenne. The ruins of his fortress, together with the priory he founded may still be seen at Castle Acre in Norfolk. Once word got out of the plot, the two earls fled to their respective castles to prepare for the coming hostilities.

William and Bishop Odo, a leading Norman warrior as well as a priest, acted quickly and decisively. Their plan, and it was a sound one militarily, was to prevent the two rebel earls uniting. Accordingly, they hurried into East Anglia and intercepted Ralph de Guader at a place called Beecham, in Norfolk. We do not know where exactly Beecham was, for there is no place of that name today. All that is clear is that the rebels were defeated and the remnants of the force, which included Earl Ralph himself, retreated to Norwich Castle to await the arrival of Roger of Hereford and his followers. Odo promptly sent a force to the Severn to hold the Hereford rebels in check, while besieging Norwich castle himself.

Norwich is a magnificent castle, right in the centre of the city, its great square keep standing on a grassy mound which always seems peaceful, despite the noise of the traffic. Unfortunately, the castle of today is not the one that was besieged by Odo. The keep, all that remains of the stonework, was not built until the twelfth century, and was entirely refaced in 1792, so that we shall never know what it actually looked like in the Middle Ages. It was evidently a strong fortress even in 1075, for it held out easily against the besiegers. But, as time passed, Ralph began to despair of Roger of Hereford coming to his aid. He managed to escape through the besiegers' lines in an effort to find help, leaving his wife in charge of the defence. Ironically, it was to the Danes, whom he had defeated outside Norwich seven years before, that he went to seek aid. They refused to become involved and the rebellion was effectively over. The siege of Norwich castle dragged on for another three months before Ralph's wife finally surrendered, though she only did so after being granted very good terms, including a safe conduct to France for herself. Once Norwich had fallen, the Earl of Hereford also surrendered.

Revolts against William Rufus

William the Conqueror died in 1087, and his possessions were split between his sons. Robert, the eldest, received Normandy, while William (nicknamed 'Rufus') succeeded to the throne of England. This was a source of contention to the barons, who would have preferred the weak, malleable Robert to the unscrupulous William. Consequently, a widespread plot was hatched to replace William by Robert, and open fighting started after Easter 1088. It is here that we meet for the first time the Bigod family, the new Earls of Norfolk, and plotters *extraordinaire*. Roger Bigod seized Norwich Castle, which had been in Crown hands since Ralph's rebellion of 1075, and terrorized the surrounding countryside. But the rebels made the mistake of waiting in their separate castles for reinforcements to come from Normandy. William began to reduce the rebel castles one by one and a naval victory, which prevented the Norman reinforcements from landing, assured him of success. Before he could begin the reduction of Norwich, the plotters surrendered.

William was lenient with the rebel leaders, but in 1095 a rebellion broke out again. The Earl of Northumberland was the leading figure in the plot, but Suffolk was represented in the person of Gilbert fitz Richard, who held the castle of Clare, which was apparently very strong. All that remains today of

Clare castle is a tall motte with the remains of two baileys. On top of the motte is a section of flint wall, dating from the thirteenth century. This castle has in fact been in ruins since the Wars of the Roses. Gilbert betrayed the plot – which involved ambushing the king on his march against Northumberland – in return for his own safety.

Castle building in stone

The reign of William's son Henry was a quiet one as far as campaigns in East Anglia go, but this period does mark the beginning of widespread castle-building in stone. The keep at Norwich, Castle Hedingham and Castle Rising are all roughly contemporary, and show similarities. Basically, the keep (which was the centre of the castle socially and militarily, and the last line of defence) was now a massive stone tower, rectangular and sheer. The walls splayed out at the bottom to resist the mines of besiegers, then rose straight up. The lower windows were few and narrow; and at Norwich there are channels built into the thickness of the wall to enable the defenders to speak to one another. The entrance to these keeps was not on the ground level, but on the first or second storey at the top of an external staircase. Often this staircase was covered by a forebuilding (such as may still be seen at Castle Rising); so that the castle keep resembled a large box with a smaller box containing the staircase on the side.

King Stephen and the period of the anarchy

When Henry died, he left two claimants to his throne. His only son had perished some years before, and it was Henry's wish that he be succeeded by his daughter Mathilda (wife of Count Geoffrey of Anjou). A number of the leading barons had sworn on oath to uphold her as rightful heir. The other claimant was Henry's nephew Stephen, Count of Blois, and the holder of vast lands in England. Although he had taken the oath upholding Mathilda, Stephen accepted the invitation of bishops and barons to claim the throne for himself. In this move he was helped by Hugh Bigod, Earl of Norfolk, who perjured himself by saying that the dying Henry had changed his mind in favour of Stephen as his successor. Stephen was also a popular choice with the Londoners.

On 22 December 1135 Stephen was crowned in

Ruins of William de Warrenne's castle at Castle Acre. William's wife was a daughter of William the Conqueror and both are perhaps better known for the priory they founded.

London after he had seized the royal coffers at Winchester. There was opposition to him, however, especially from Robert, Earl of Gloucester, who was in fact an illegitimate son of Henry. Trouble was soon to flare up, even though the Earl of Gloucester came to terms with Stephen at the beginning of April 1136. For that very month an inexplicable rumour somehow began that Stephen had died, and this went round the kingdom like wildfire, sparking off a series of petty baronial revolts that mark the beginning of the disturbances that were to last for the rest of the reign.

Hugh Bigod was the first to revolt and he seized Norwich Castle. Stephen in person had to lead an army into Norfolk before Bigod would give up his prize. Then there was a revolt in Devon, another in Hampshire, and yet a third which led to Bedford Castle being besieged by Stephen in the midwinter of 1138. Even when the kingdom was peaceful internally, there was the problem of the Scots on the northern borders of England. This was serious enough to warrant a campaign by Stephen during the summer of 1138. Even when the Scots had been beaten there was no peace for Stephen. Hereford-

shire had to be put down, then Bristol and Chester rose against him. So it went on, month after month, until the end of September 1139, when Stephen, besieging Marlborough castle, received word that his rival for the throne, Mathilda, had landed in Sussex and taken shelter in Arundel castle. With her was her brother, Robert of Gloucester, who was to figure as her most capable general in the coming years. Stephen at once marched to Arundel, almost capturing Robert en route, and besieged it. Then, for some totally inexplicable reason, he allowed Mathilda to go in safety to Bristol to join her

An old engraving of Norwich Castle. Norwich was the scene of one of the first baronial revolts against William the Conqueror. The Earls of Norfolk and Hereford hatched their plot during the wedding feast of Hereford's sister and Norfolk.

brother. It was a decision that was to cost him dear. For, with his rival personally in the field, the rebellions assumed the character of a civil war. It was a conflict that was to drag on for fifteen years.

War came to East Anglia soon after this. Hugh Bigod's father, Roger, had built a castle at Bungay, which had been taken by the Crown – no doubt as punishment for Bigod involvement in one of the various plots already mentioned. Bungay lies west of Lowestoft, in a loop of the River Waveney, and commands one of the major water routes into the hinterland of East Anglia. Its loss was a shock to Stephen, who believed that all the castles of the east and south of England were in the hands of those he could trust, and that his major problem lay in the west. Consequently, he immediately mounted an expedition and captured the castle. We do not know exactly what happened, but evidently the lesson was

All this time, Mathilda had been freely granting titles and honours to her followers. Among those who benefited was Geoffrey de Mandeville. He was not only confirmed as Constable of the Tower of London, but was also made Earl of Essex. Geoffrey was a self-seeking man, entirely out for his own ends, and quite content to play the two sides off against each other if it appeared to be to his advantage to do so. In December 1141, he was approached by Stephen, who wanted to buy his support. Geoffrey's price was high – not only did Stephen have to confirm all the titles which Geoffrey had received from Mathilda; he had also to grant him the right to raise a new castle wherever he pleased on his own lands. (In this age, a prospective castle builder had to obtain the king's permission, though of course this law was frequently flouted during the civil wars.) In return, Geoffrey marched with Stephen in the spring of 1142 to put down the insurgents in the Isle of Ely.

The rebels, meanwhile, were concentrating round Oxford, and holding the Severn Valley. They were in desperate straits, however, and it was this that led them to deal with the cunning Geoffrey of Essex again. Robert of Gloucester had seen that if Geoffrey could be swung to the rebel cause, then Stephen would have to divide his time and energy against two fronts; always a difficult and perilous situation to be in. So once again Geoffrey started bargaining. This time he received confirmation of the possession of the castle that Stephen had allowed him to build (this was on the River Lea), plus the right to build another. In addition, he also wanted the right to occupy or destroy the castle of the Bishop of London at Stortford (in Hereford-shire) because it interfered with his communications between the Tower and his castles in Essex. At the same time, Geoffrey's brother-in-law, Aubrey de Vere, was to be made Earl of Cambridge and to have possession of Colchester castle.

It was a good bargain, but it was one that was not to benefit Geoffrey. For that was the year of Stephen's best campaign. He was able to win a series of victories, culminating in the capture of Oxford. Mathilda herself was at Oxford, and escaped only by being lowered from the walls in the middle of the night. So Geoffrey dared not move on his own, and the time for striking passed. If Mathilda had been free and able to support him, he might have done something. As it was he sat tight and kept his peace with Stephen. The latter knew of the treachery, but bided his time before making a move. In September 1143, while he was at St

lost on Bigod, who rebelled again in August, and against whom another punitive force had to be sent. This was enough to bring the earl over to the king's side, and the very next year saw Bigod and William de Warrenne, the other great East Anglian noble, commanding the right wing of Stephen's army at the battle of Lincoln, fought on 2 February 1141. It was not a particularly glorious occasion for the two East Anglians. They had quarrelled bitterly with other barons over the command of the right wing, and the result was a hopelessly confused chain of command. When the rebel left advanced, the royalist men-at-arms lowered lances and went forward to meet them. Suddenly the rebel heavy cavalry burst into their ranks, hacking down the foot soldiers, and causing a panic that swept away Stephen's right wing, and with it any hopes of victory.

Albans, he had Geoffrey arrested, and once again he offered Geoffrey a bargain. This one was quite simple – Geoffrey could either deliver up his castles at Pleshey, Saffron Walden and the Tower of London, or be hung. Of the two Essex castles, little remains. At Pleshey, near Chelmsford, there is still a motte fifty feet high, a moat with a fifteenth-century bridge, and a large outer bailey that takes in much of the village. In Saffron Walden, the few remains of the castle are in Church Street, where the ruined flint walls of the keep are visible. Adjoining is an interesting museum.

Geoffrey was not the man to allow such indignities to go unavenged. Once at liberty, he gathered together a band of tough desperadoes like himself, and retired into the Fens, emerging only to rob and pillage. He was a shrewd general, and proved to be adept at guerrilla operations. Fordham, which lies just inside Cambridgeshire (five miles north of the A45 near Newmarket), was his first base. It was convenient for raiding Suffolk and also, via the Icknield Way, Essex and Hertfordshire. Fordham was only temporary, however, for eight miles to the northwest lies Ely. Today Ely is a fair city in a drained fertile plain; then it was an island in a trackless swamp. Not only did it possess two of the Conqueror's castles – Ely and Aldreth – but it had also recently revolted against Stephen. There, Geoffrey felt sure, he would be welcomed; and in November 1143, he occupied the Isle without opposition. In addition, the leading barons of East Anglia were conveniently neutral, and he had the active support of many of his tenants in Essex.

The massive keep of Colchester Castle is built on the foundations of the Roman temple of Claudius. It was built on the orders of William the Conqueror and is the largest Norman keep in Britain other than the White Tower of the Tower of London.

Like all good guerrilla leaders, he realized that to stay on the defensive would be fatal and so, within a month of taking Ely, he was ready to mount his first offensive operation. This time, his target was the monastery at Ramsey, fifteen miles west of Ely. At this period, as we saw, a number of castles were still of the earth and timber variety, so the capture of a stone monastery gave Geoffrey the nucleus of a potentially strong fortress. He ejected the monks and set to work strengthening the defences, secure in the knowledge that the western approaches to the Isle of Ely were now safe from surprise attack. He still took precautions to improve his position by establishing two further posts: at Wood Walton (Huntingdonshire) which lies west of Ramsey, just off the modern A1; and at Benwick, five miles north-east of Ramsey. Wood Walton is a low ringwork, with a ditch that encloses the natural hilltop that formed the strongpoint of the position. Nothing is known about Wood Walton, but Ramsey does have a few remains. The abbey itself has disappeared, although some of the stones in the wall of the churchyard were part of that building. There are still traces of the breastwork and ditch that Geoffrey built, and there is also a mound surrounded by a further ditch on the south side of the abbey.

A glance at the map shows the strength of Geoffrey's holdings. Behind the Ouse and the Fens lay his two castles in the Isle of Ely. His weak west flank was protected by Ramsey, which could be approached only after the two outer works, Wood Walton and Benwick, had been reduced. In the east, Fordham castle enabled him to keep in touch with his supporters in Essex.

With his band growing every day, Geoffrey was soon to start a reign of terror in the region. Cambridge was the first to suffer. Although there was a castle there, the defence was passive. While Geoffrey was unable to reduce the castle itself, the garrison was quite unable to prevent the town from being thoroughly sacked. Even the churches were not immune from the lawless raiders who pursued their victims to the altar steps, recognizing no sanctuary. When the looting was over, the town was given up to the torch and burned.

Stephen came to put an end to Geoffrey's atrocities in the spring of 1144, and found the task to be more difficult than he had anticipated. Geoffrey refused to meet him in the open, and withdrew into the Fens where the land itself would aid him. To us in the twentieth century, with our memories of Viet Nam, the course of Geoffrey's campaign follows a familiar pattern. While Stephen's

Bungay Castle was the second most important of the Bigod castles. The conflict between Hugh Bigod and Henry II gave rise to the old Suffolk nursery rhyme:
> Were I in my castle of Bungay
>> By the waters of Waveney,
> I would ne care
>> For the king of Cockneye.

forces floundered blindly in the swamps, the rebels played a deadly game of catch-as-catch-can: avoiding, ambushing, slipping away, re-appearing in the royalist rear; never fighting equal numbers, but delivering swift, stinging attacks incessantly. Not surprisingly, Stephen withdrew.

Stephen had many good qualities as a soldier, though he is one of our least-known kings. Possibly this is because he spent his whole reign fighting other Englishmen, rather than winning possessions abroad. At any rate, once defeated, he changed his strategy. He had been pushed out of the Fens. It seemed unlikely that Geoffrey could be dislodged easily, so Stephen decided to erect a chain of castles that would contain him. These were at Sapley (in Huntingdonshire), Knapwell, Rampton, Burwell (Cambridgeshire), Weeting (Norfolk), and Freckenham (Suffolk). All these were simple earth and timber structures except Burwell, which belonged to the Earls of Worcester, and all of them except Burwell have disappeared, save for a shallow ditch at Weeting, which encloses a rectangular area and large mound. This lies north of the village itself,

down a lane that runs from the B1106 in the village centre. Of the castles, Burwell and Freckenham were the most important; they lie five miles southeast (on the B1202) and north-west of Fordham. Their function was to prevent Geoffrey communicating with or receiving help from East Anglia.

Geoffrey made a few probes to test the strength of these positions, but found them too strong to take. Like all guerrillas, he had adopted a policy of living off what he captured from his enemies. Now, thrown back on his own resources, his difficulties began. He requisitioned all the food in the Isle of Ely, so that the poor died of starvation and lay unburied in the fields. Those that resisted his demands had their homes burned, and he gradually lost the support of the inhabitants who had once welcomed him with open arms.

By the end of the summer, Geoffrey was in a desperate position. So critical had it become that he gambled everything on one last effort to break out and communicate with his East Anglian supporters. Burwell was chosen as the target for the attempt to break the stranglehold, and throughout August the rebels began to congregate there in preparation for the assault. The remains of Burwell castle lie to the east of the village, behind the church in the main street, and can be reached best by taking the lane down the side of the church. All that can be seen now is a rectangular mound surrounded by a wide, shallow ditch. Excavations have shown that there was once a thick curtain wall faced with flint, with a square gate house. Across the moat ran a wooden bridge. It was here that Geoffrey was to die. As he was reconnoitring the castle, he was careless enough to remove his helmet, and was struck by a stray arrow. Dying slowly of his gangrenous wound, he was taken to Mildenhall Abbey. With his loss, the heart went out of the rebels. For a while, the dead Geoffrey's son hung on to Ramsey Abbey. The abbot himself was conspicuous in its recapture; he personally set alight to the fortified outer gate and the tents of the rebels. After this, peace came again to East Anglia, though the war dragged on in other parts of the kingdom.

Nine years passed, and then the peace was broken by the machinations of the wily Hugh Bigod. Little is known of what he was actually planning, but the centre of trouble was the Bigod castle at Ipswich.

The modern visitor to Ipswich might wonder at this, for today there is no trace of a castle. The site of the castle is not known, though earthworks in the Arboretum grounds of Christ Church Mansion may be the Bigod fortress; or the mount near St Stephen's church may be the site. A third location has been suggested at Cox Lane, where excavations uncovered a sizeable ditch and large mortared stone blocks.

Wherever the castle was, Stephen and his son Eustace came to besiege it in 1153. In August, Eustace was harrying the country around Bury St Edmunds; but on his return to the siege lines at Ipswich he caught a fever, and died in camp shortly after. The town fell, but this was nothing compared to the damage that Eustace's death did to Stephen's cause. This was almost the last act of the war, for Stephen accepted Henry, Duke of Normandy, as his successor. Henry had been the new hope of Stephen's opponents since the departure of Mathilda to the Continent in 1148, after the death of Robert of Gloucester. Stephen died in 1154 and Duke Henry, who was to reign until 1189, became King Henry II.

Henry II

The first task of the new king was the restoration of law and order to a realm weary of war. During Stephen's reign, large numbers of unlicensed castles had been built. Some of them, such as Saffron Walden, had been partially demolished, but others proved to be a problem. Henry was a tough man who determined to have his way, and his first orders were that all Crown lands were to be restored to the Crown. To support this order, he marched into the Midlands and Lincolnshire, and so overawed the barons by his display of force that even Hugh Bigod was forced to obey him.

East Anglia worried the king. Hugh Bigod had a monopoly of power there, and Hugh was a plotter second to none; certainly he was not to be trusted. An open rebellion in the north diverted Henry's attention for a time but by 1157 he was ready to do something about the East Anglian situation. He held the Whitsun court at Bury St Edmunds, and among those who attended were William of Boulogne and Hugh Bigod. The former, a son of King Stephen, was the owner of vast lands and held Norwich castle. Once he had the two in his power, Henry somehow put pressure on them to give up their unlicensed castles, and thus got control of Norwich again.

Castle Rising Castle, Norfolk, like Castle Hedingham, shows the early stone style of castle construction. This massive square keep was the social centre of the complex and was designed as the 'last ditch' defence.

For twenty years there was peace in the kingdom, although Henry was preparing for the revolt that he knew must eventually break out against his efforts to increase the power of the Crown. This period is therefore a very interesting one from the point of view of the strategy which lay behind his preparations. We are particularly fortunate in that a great deal of contemporary evidence survives, in the shape of the Pipe Rolls. The Pipe Rolls are the Exchequer Records, made up year by year to detail the king's spending. Examination of them provides a fascinating guide to Henry's policy. Over the twenty years, 1154–74, we see the king gradually taking over the defence of the realm. With Crown revenue constantly increasing, the king was able to undertake projects which the barons simply could not afford to imitate. In 1158, there was a great deal of expenditure on castles and garrisons: Norwich garrison received £51.12s., while Walton (Suffolk) garrison was paid the huge sum of £96.12s.8d. £9.12s.4d. was set aside to complete the destruction of Saffron Walden castle.

At this time, too, Henry was building a number of new royal castles at strategic places. Consider his strategy in Suffolk. In 1154, there was not one royal castle in the whole county. Bigod had a monopoly, with strongholds at Framlingham (the main Bigod lair), Bungay, Walton and Thetford. By the bold stroke of policy of 1157, Henry got them all, and Norwich and Eye as well. In 1165, he gave back Framlingham and Bungay, but kept Thetford and Walton, hence their constant appearance in the Pipe Rolls.

Bigod, meanwhile, was strengthening Bungay. It is his castle that constitutes the ruins which can be seen today behind the King's Head Hotel. All that now remain are fragments of curtain wall, and a gatehouse guarded by two rounded towers. The keep was rectangular, built of Caen stone and faced with sandstone. Entry to the keep was via the forebuilding on the south side. It was a strong castle, but it was one that Henry could ignore. The Pipe Rolls tell us why Henry could let Bigod have two castles back; that year, 1165, two thirds of the king's spending on defence (£600 out of a total of £900) was on one item – a new superfortress at Orford in Suffolk.

Orford Castle, Suffolk, is one of the best preserved and most unusual castles in England. Its polygonal plan gave it immense strength. It was built by Henry II with the strategic purpose of cutting off Framlingham Castle from the sea.

Orford is one of the most interesting castles in the whole of England, and it is almost perfectly preserved. It represents the very latest fashion in military architecture of its age, and was designed to be stronger than anything that Bigod could hope to build. In shape it is polygonal – having no sharp angles to invite attack – and it is circular inside. The walls are further strengthened by three great buttress towers that are built on the outside of the keep on every fifth face. The door, on the second storey, gives into the great hall, while in one tower there is a spiral staircase, with sleeping chambers in the other two. A deep well in the basement provided water. There were once outer walls, but these have fallen down over the ages. Orford today is a sleepy village, full of pleasure boats and yachts. When Henry built his castle, it was a thriving port, and could be supplied by sea in an emergency. It was also sited to interdict communications with Framlingham, which stands on a tributary of the Alde. Orford castle is best approached from Woodbridge on the B1084, and is well worth a visit.

Orford cost the staggering sum of £1,400, and was completed in 1173. That same year the rebellion that Henry had anticipated broke out. Henry, by his marriage, had acquired vast territories in France. Not unnaturally, Louis VII of France hated to see these in England's hands, and plotted to overthrow Henry. Embroiled in the plot were Henry's eldest son (also called Henry), Malcolm of Scotland, and a number of the English barons, including, inevitably, Hugh Bigod. Bigod's price was the castles of Norwich and Eye.

This was the moment that Henry had been planning for, and it is appropriate to note his achievements here. Over the whole kingdom, he had no less than twenty-three modern or strengthened castles on which to base his defence. In East Anglia, he owned Colchester, Norwich and Orford, all of which stood on or near the old Roman road into our region. In Norwich, he had the local administration of the area under his control and although Bungay cut it off from London, he in turn had cut off Framlingham from the coast.

In April 1173, the rebellion flared up. Henry himself was in Normandy, which was also in arms against him, and he was so occupied there that the defeat of the English rebels had to be left to the devices of the two Justiciars. These two, Earl Reginald of Cornwall and Richard de Lucy acted wisely and well. The old castle at Cambridge was refortified, and Thetford, lying as it does on that important Norwich–Cambridge road, was quickly

garrisoned. Aldreth, Wisbech and Eye, all motte and bailey structures, were made ready and stocked with men and provisions. A glance at the map shows the Justiciars' plan. Hugh Bigod had been cut off from the Midland rebels by a 'cordon sanitaire' of castles. There in the north is Wisbech, then Aldreth, Cambridge, Hertford and London. Hugh was further confined by a fortified line running east and west, from Thetford to Bury, Eye, Haughley, Ipswich and Walton on the coast. South of that lay Colchester. Even supposing that Hugh had been able to take Colchester, he would still have faced the almost impossible task of crossing the Thames below London in the face of opposition from the Tower.

Help was coming, however, from overseas. On 29 September, Robert, Earl of Leicester, landed in the Orwell estuary with a force of French and Flemish mercenaries. Very wisely, he left Walton Castle, which stood a mile and a half north of the Orwell and has since vanished beneath the sea, completely alone. His first task was to get to Hugh's fortress at Framlingham, and once there the two leaders made plans to break out of the ring of fortified places that so restricted their movements. In the meantime, the French and Flemish soldiers were committing terrible atrocities in their search for loot. On 13 October, the rebels came to attack Haughley. It is today the largest earthwork in Suffolk; then it was a strong motte and bailey castle owned by Ranulf de Broc. It was unable to survive the weight of attack that was directed against it, and was taken by assault that same day. The two moated enclosures and the eighty-foot high mound are all that can be seen of the castle which the rebels destroyed.

Haughley lies midway between two towns, Ipswich and Bury. The rebels intended to march west, by-pass Bury, and then march down the Icknield Way, using the old Roman road to Cambridge, the capture of which would have given them a clear march to Leicester. They were anxious to avoid Bury because of the heavy reinforcements which had arrived there. When Henry's Justiciar, Richard de Lucy, heard of the landing in the Orwell, he hurried back from the Scots border. With him were three hundred of Henry's stipendiary knights, but he was pitifully weak in infantry. Leicester and the rebels, on the other hand, had plenty of seasoned infantry, but little cavalry. The royalists flung themselves into Bury to await the rebels.

In view of the large numbers of knights in Bury,

Robert of Leicester behaved with astonishing care-
lessness. Instead of taking precautions, his troops
were allowed to stay in a casual route-march
formation, and as they marched they sang derisive
songs about the English. A mile north of Bury, on
the modern A134, lie the three Fornham villages – St
Genevieve, St Martin and All Saints. Through
them flows the River Lark, a marshy stream with
water meadows on either side. Richard de Lucy was
watching the rebels from the walls of Bury, and saw
his chance. For as the rebel army attempted the
crossing of the Lark, it became split into two parts
by the river. The heavy knights came storming out
of Bury, utterly overwhelming the small body of
horsemen which the rebels had, and capturing
Robert of Leicester himself. Then they fell on the
disorganized French and Flemings, riding them
down in the meadows which look so peaceful today.
Worse was to follow for the mercenaries. Their
atrocities had so incensed the local country folk that
numbers of peasants, armed only with pitchforks
and flails, had joined the king's forces. It was they
who completed the rout of the Flemings – pursuing
them in the marshy ground where armoured knights

This print of Orford Castle shows the keep and
the last surviving fragment of the bailey wall
which has now been pulled down and the
material carried away for local building.

would have been bogged down. In their hatred they
were implacable, and large numbers of the foreigners
died terrible deaths inflicted by those primitive
weapons.

The success of the royalists was complete, and
they exploited it. Extra garrisons were sent up to
Bury, Ipswich and Colchester in a display of force
designed to show Hugh Bigod that he could not
hope to win. Hugh was forced to accept this, and
negotiated a truce to last until Easter 1174, at the
same time dismissing from his service those few
Flemings who were still alive. The royalists could
possibly have got better terms by further action
against Hugh, but the situation was critical on the
Scottish border, and Richard de Lucy was quite
happy to have even a temporary respite in East
Anglia.

When the truce ran out it was essential for the
rebels to strike the first blow. They simply had to

break out of the ring of castles, and this applied to the Midland rebels as well as Hugh Bigod. On 15 May 1174, help for the rebels arrived. The Orwell once again saw the landing of numbers of Flemish mercenaries, who joined Hugh at Framlingham. This time they began by attempting to take over the local administration at Norwich. At first, they had some success, and stormed the town, But the sight of that lofty stone keep, which still looms over the city, was too much for them. They had not the heart for an assault; for a formal siege, they had neither time nor resources. On 18 June, they quietly drifted away.

Hugh next tried to get a fortified base on the coast by attacking Dunwich. The village of Dunwich has now been swallowed by the sea, and we have no records of what was actually there for Hugh to assault. We do know that this effort too failed, leaving Hugh in a desperate situation. No matter how he tried, he simply could not break out of East Anglia, and though he was quite free to pillage and loot, this made absolutely no difference to the strategic situation.

Meanwhile, elsewhere the struggle was going well for Henry. The Scots king himself had been captured, the Midland rebels had taken a terrific pounding at Henry's hands, and a full scale siege of Huntingdon was in progress. On 21 July, Henry received the surrender of that city, and was left with a free hand to settle accounts with Hugh Bigod. He advanced straight on the Bigod fortress at Framlingham with a strong army which included 500 carpenters to make the siege engines. They were not needed, for on 25 July, Hugh came out and surrendered. It needed a full scale siege to reduce Bungay, the other Bigod fortress, which was defended by some 500 men. The king's sappers managed to drive a mine under the south-west corner of the keep, and this probably induced the garrison to surrender. Mining was a typical operation in medieval siege warfare. The technique was to drive a shaft under the castle wall, using large quantities of timber to prop up the sides and roof. When the timber was lit, the mine shaft collapsed, often bringing down the wall with it. Excavations in 1891 turned up the mine at Bungay, which runs from the west wall to the prison under the forebuilding. Bungay was devastated in this siege, and was in ruins until 1294, when a new work was erected on the site.

Henry's achievements in East Anglia should not be underrated. In twenty years the balance of power in terms of castles had been completely upset, and

the Bigod monopoly was destroyed. Hugh was fined 1,000 marks for his part in the insurrection, and lost Framlingham and Bungay. In the Pipe Rolls we find that 'Alnoth the Engineer' and 'carpenters and masons' received £13.15s.11d. for destroying Framlingham, plus 36s. 1d. for filling in the moat. With Bigod gone, the king could afford to cut his expenditure by destroying his own castle at Ipswich the same year, and selling the stores and equipment in Walton Castle. But this was not to be the end of the Bigods; for after Henry's death and the death of Hugh, Framlingham was to be rebuilt, and pose problems for another English king.

King John and the barons

Richard the Lion Heart, who followed Henry, was always beset by financial troubles. In his attempts to raise revenue he went so far as to say that he would sell London itself, if only he could find a buyer. It was through the king's desire for revenue that the Bigods were able to pay to get Framlingham back.

There was peace during Richard's reign, but the accession of his brother, John, was the signal for a fresh outbreak of hostility between Crown and nobility. It was in fact in Bury St Edmunds that the barons took their oath to seek the constitutional changes embodied in the Magna Carta. The signing of that document at Runnymede in 1215 is usually regarded as a victory for the barons. So it was, but neither side expected the agreement to last long, and both parties were preparing for war throughout the autumn and winter of 1215. Geoffrey, Earl of Essex was the leader of a group of plotters who invited Louis, eldest son of the king of France, to reign in John's place. The first contingent of the French army landed in the Orwell and marched through Essex into London, where they settled down to spend the winter in luxury and idleness. John in the meantime was far from idle. Before Christmas, he besieged and took Bedford, which surrendered when the garrison despaired of the barons mounting a relief operation. Then, near St Albans on 20 December, he split his army into two parts; one part was to march with him to Nottingham to settle affairs there, the other was to watch the French in London and occupy East Anglia.

Opposite Castle Hedingham was besieged and taken by King John, whose mercenaries ransacked the building. Originally the staircase seen in the picture would have been enclosed and protected by a forebuilding.

Castle Rising Castle, Norfolk. This different view shows the size of the building. Eventually only the Crown could build castles of this size and in any number, owing to the very substantial cost.

The barons were inactive. They had formed the impression that John would be beaten only by a French army led personally by Louis. Unfortunately for them, Louis had other pressing business in France, and kept postponing his voyage to England – though he did send a second heavy contingent of men at the beginning of the New Year, 1216.

From Hampshire, the royal army under Savaric de Mauleon and Falkes de Breaute, moved into East Anglia. From the Icknield Way, they drove the rebels out of Bury and chased them north into the Isle of Ely, which they devastated. With Cambridgeshire, Norfolk and Suffolk overrun, de Mauleon left a force to watch the Isle of Ely, and probed down towards Colchester. He had flung a loose cordon round the place when a force of French mercenaries came up from London to the relief. De Mauleon

interpreted this as a sign that the whole baronial army was on the move, and retreated north to Ely. In fact he was mistaken, and the bulk of the rebel forces remained in London.

By the end of February, John was master of all England, save for a few East Anglian castles, and it was to these that he now turned his attention. In March he was ready to attack the centre of East Anglian rebellion: Roger Bigod's castle at Framlingham. We have already seen that the fortress destroyed by Henry II had been recovered by the Bigods. It had been completely rebuilt, and the sight that faced John would not be much different from the one which faces the modern visitor today.

The castle at Framlingham dates from around 1200. It is the finest in Suffolk, and arguably one of the best in East Anglia. From the point of view of historical associations, it is unsurpassed; for almost every plot in the Middle Ages included the treacherous, double-dealing Bigods of Framlingham. The architectural style of the keeps at Colchester and

Hedingham has already been mentioned. They were great rectangular towers, whose weakness lay in the sharp corners which invited attack. Orford, also a tower, was polygonal, representing an improvement over the square style. Framlingham is a good example of the next step forward again – the shell keep. These keeps are larger, and are not towers but heavily fortified inner wards, open to the sky, consisting of a curtain wall interspersed with towers to give flanking fire. The style was in fact a copy of the Roman design, which featured round towers set in the wall. Framlingham has thirteen towers around the keep.

The castle site is on an old Saxon burial ground and, legend has it, fortress. The inner ward is very well preserved, and has a forty-four foot wall, set with towers, and a deep moat. There was an outer bailey (where the town now is) which itself had a moat, while over to the west was a smaller lower ward, protected by the damming of the river Ore, which produced an artificial marsh. The castle lay

Framlingham, home of the Bigods, Earls of Norfolk. It was Roger the 5th Earl's refusal to serve with the English army which prompted Edward I's famous pun : 'By God Earl, you shall either serve or be hanged'. In fact, Roger Bigod did neither.

in an angle of the town ditch, and had a two-storey great hall inside the inner ward.

Bigod was in a position of great strength, but seems not to have had the determination to go with his defences. As soon as John appeared, on 12 March, he surrendered. This easy victory encouraged John to take action against the other strongholds that still held out against him. On 13 March he was at Ipswich, and the next day he was in front of Colchester.

Colchester had caused John problems before. William de Lauvalei had held it, but John distrusted him, and had replaced him by Stephen Harengoot. Trouble was brewing and the castle, which had had a new bailey built in 1173-4 as part of Henry's programme against Bigod, was strengthened by John. He sent eight ballistae, large siege engines designed to shoot heavy iron javelins, to the castle from London. As part of the settlement at the signing of the Magna Carta, Lauvelei was restored to his fortress but he joined the rebellion which followed. When John came up against it, Colchester was garrisoned by the French who had landed in the Orwell, and the rebel Earl of Winchester was also present.

The French were disinclined to resist, and promised surrender on two conditions. The first was that they be allowed to go free, the second was that the English part of the garrison should be held for ransom and not hanged out of hand. John agreed, but once he had possession of the castle, he put the English in chains. When the French got back to London, the barons angrily accused them of betraying their comrades, and threatened to execute them. But the French were instead kept in custody until Louis himself arrived to decide their fate.

On 25 March 1216, John was on the move again, this time to Hedingham in Essex, where the Earl of Oxford held the castle for the barons. Hedingham is a magnificent (though relatively unknown) castle, and is well worth a visit. It lies on the A604, Colchester to Cambridge road, four miles north of Halstead. The castle is a square tower keep of Northamptonshire stone. It was built about 1130, and has a basement and three storeys which rise to 1,100 feet, with two twenty-foot towers on top. At the base, the walls are twelve feet thick with tiny arrow-slit windows. The entrance is on the first storey, with an external staircase along the west wall, giving access to the forebuilding which has now disappeared. Outside the keep are the remains of a moat and outer ward wall which originally enclosed about three acres. In its day it was one of the strongest fortresses in England, and had been seized from the Crown by the Earl of Oxford in 1214. After a siege of three days, it surrendered, and the Earl came out and threw himself on John's mercy.

This was another blow for the barons, who were now beginning to lose heart. John had captured a

Framlingham Castle—a view showing the great wall of the original castle which was confiscated by Henry II and destroyed. The walls were rebuilt c. 1200. *Overleaf* Middiman's engraving of Framlingham Castle. Stone for the castle was brought by boat up the river Ore which, today, is no more than a marshy stream.

great deal of his enemies' property, and stopped at Hedingham to share out the loot before making a final march on London. In the face of this, the barons were almost ready to surrender. It was only Louis who stopped them. He sent over the third contingent of his army, and promised to appear in person by Easter, which fell on 10 April. It was this that persuaded the barons to hold out – though, in fact, Louis still had not arrived by Easter.

When John got news of Louis' impending arrival, he was forced to change his plans. On 14 April he ordered twenty-one coastal towns, including King's Lynn, Yarmouth and Dunwich, to send their ships to the mouth of the Thames to intercept Louis. John himself led his army to the Kent coast, expecting that this would be the most likely landing area. When he discovered that Louis had not left France, he decided to use the ships which he had impressed into his service to blockade Calais, so that Louis would have to fight his way out. It was a good plan, and sound strategy, but fate took a hand. As the fleet was gathering off Dover on 18 May, it was struck by a sudden squall which sank a number of vessels and scattered the rest.

Louis seized his chance and dashed over two days later. He landed in Kent, almost within sight of John. John did not dare fight because a large part of his army consisted of French mercenaries who technically owed allegiance to Louis, and who therefore might show an inclination to desert. He was compelled to retreat, first to Hampshire, then to the borders of Wales, while Louis was received with jubilation in London. Among the leading barons who came to do him homage was De Warrenne of Castle Acre. The baronial forces and their French allies meanwhile swept north out of London into East Anglia, burning, devastating and looting.

Louis and his ally, Alexander of Scotland, were attempting to reduce two of the strongest royalist castles: Windsor and Dover. While the former was besieged by a baronial army, the two monarchs drew the siege lines around Dover. John had two aims. He knew that Dover would be safe for a while, but was worried about Windsor. He wanted to raise the siege there but, more important, he knew also that Alexander would be returning to Scotland, and he wanted to capture him. To this end, he decided to ambush the Scot somewhere in East Anglia.

From the borders of Wales, he made a lightning march to Windsor. It was early September and, as night fell, his archers reconnoitred the rebel camp. It was too strong to take: instead the archers sent clouds of arrows whistling out of the darkness to create havoc among the rebels. While they were still in a state of shock, John marched rapidly away towards East Anglia. The barons did exactly what he had intended. Having sorted out the confusion, they realized that John was near and raised the siege in order to pursue him. John had thus accomplished his first object of relieving Windsor.

With the barons pursuing him, John reached

An early cannon from Castle Rising Castle. The development of gunpowder in the High Middle Ages spelt the deathknell of the castle.

Opposite Caister. One of the last military actions of the Middle Ages took place here when, in the Wars of the Roses, the castle was besieged.

Cambridge on 15 September. The barons hoped to bring him to battle there, but John was too wily to be caught. He knew of their approach and made a sudden, and brilliantly-executed, night march south to Clare and then to Hedingham. This completely baffled the barons and threw them off the track. They contented themselves with ravaging Cambridgeshire and then drifted south to join Louis at Dover. John marched up to Stamford.

Alexander of Scotland, meanwhile had reached Cambridge. His next stop was to be Lincoln, which was in rebel hands. It was unfortunate for John that he had not remained waiting for Alexander. Instead, he had decided to punish all East Anglian rebels, and was burning Peterborough, Oundle and Crowland. At the latter place, he ordered Savaric de Mauleon to burn the monastery. De Mauleon was so affected by the pleas of the monks that he spared the buildings for ransom. When he returned to John, the king was furious. Heaping abuse on his trusted lieutenant, he seized a burning brand himself and, like a madman, ran cursing through the ripe corn, setting it alight. Even as he did so, Alexander was eluding him. Lincolnshire was taught the same lesson as East Anglia, and John did not return to Lincoln until 28 September. There, he learned that the Scots had dodged him and were safely in Yorkshire. John promptly forgot about Alexander in his mad desire to punish the remaining centres of insurgency in East Anglia. Burning and looting, he came to King's Lynn on 9 October. He was enthusiastically received, and began to fortify it.

It was while he was there that he caught dysentery. Though ill, he seemed unable to rest, and marched on to Wisbech on the 11th. There, his raging mind drove him on again to the mouth of the Welland. Beyond reason or advice, he set out to cross the treacherous salt marshes of the Wash, without waiting for either guides or ebb tide. As the army sloshed across the great expanse of brackish water, the ground began to slip and open. John got away, so did a few of his knights: but of his army, his spare horses, his equipment and his treasure, there was no sign. He was fevered, and his mind was further tortured by the news that the garrison of Dover had been compelled to ask for a truce. That night he gorged himself on peaches and raw cider, which worsened his condition. Next day, moaning in his pain, he was carried in a litter to Newark.

Today, if you avoid the by-pass and travel through the town, you can still see the ruins of the castle of the Bishop of Lincoln looking down on the River Trent. It was there that John lay three days

dying. It had been a bad reign, the troubles epitomized by the grim little procession that took the king's body without ceremony through the bleak winter landscape to Worcester. A contemporary chronicler has perhaps left the most terrible epitaph that any king has had: 'Forasmuch when he came to die he possessed none of his land in peace, he is called John Lackland.'

The last of medieval warfare

John was succeeded by his son, Henry III, who was a boy of nine. The kingdom which he inherited was half in enemy hands. Our region was completely occupied by Louis, except for the castles of Norwich, Orford, Colchester, Hedingham and Pleshey, and Cambridgeshire, which was held by the ruthless Falkes de Breaute. The new king himself held only the Midlands, and was supported by the Earls of Chester, Derby and Pembroke. During the first six months of his reign, the royalists were on the defensive. They had to buy time, and offered Louis Norwich and Orford in return for a truce. At the beginning of 1217, Louis and his followers met in Cambridge and decided that there would be no peace settlement. Hedingham was besieged again, and a further truce was arranged in exchange for the surrender of Colchester and Hedingham.

Louis had to return to France on urgent business, and his cause began to fail. Falkes de Breaute took the Isle of Ely, and all the time adherents were joining the royalist cause. This was because now the English had a king who had made no enemies. The royalists won such a magnificent victory in April 1217 at Lincoln that Louis was led to seek peace. He was still hoping for reinforcements from France, but the defeat of his fleet in the Channel in August was a blow which ended all hopes of victory for him, and Henry was accepted as king.

This marked the end of medieval warfare in East Anglia. It is perhaps a sign of the times that Falkes de Breaute was besieged in Bedford castle in 1224 and hanged for behaving with the high-handedness and lawlessness that was so common in John's reign. Of course, there are still many interesting facts which could be mentioned about East Anglian castles after 1217, but they are not truly military episodes. For instance, there was a widespread revolt in East Anglia in 1381, when the Essex men

Great Yarmouth. One of sixteen towers built by the town to the command of Henry III in 1260. The object was to encircle the town with a wall.

marched on London and dispersed only at the persuasion of the boy-king, Richard II. But mainly the fighting of the High Middle Ages is confined to the Welsh Marches, Scotland or France. There are links between East Anglia and the glories of that age, but they are tenuous ones. Mettingham in Suffolk, for instance, was built when the owner, Sir John de Norwich, was given a license to crenellate as reward for his conduct at the great naval battle of Sluys.

One last incident that is worthy of mention dates from the time of the Wars of the Roses in the mid-fifteenth century. Many nobles took advantage of the general disorders to pay off old scores and settle grudges by force. This is what happened at Caister in 1469. At a point four miles north of Yarmouth, on the modern A1064, Sir John Fastolf built a castle in 1450 from the ransom of a French knight whom he had captured at Agincourt. It passed to John Paston, but was claimed by John Mowbray, Duke of Norfolk. He attacked it in 1469 with 3,000 men, but incredibly the thirty defenders held him off, and only gave up the struggle when the Duke brought up reinforcements from King's Lynn. Paston regained the castle eight years later.

But this is the last medieval episode of note in East Anglia. Sixteen years later, at Bosworth Field, East Anglians were present at the battle which marks the end of the Middle Ages and the beginning of the Tudor Age.

Kett the tanner harangues insurgents under the Oak of Reformation at Mousehold Hill near Norwich. Kett's rebellion was quashed by a battle with Italian mercenaries in the pay of the Crown at St Andrew's Plain, Norwich. The engraving, by Sparrow, was published in 1792.

5

THE TUDOR AGE

WITH the accession of Henry VII, the Middle Ages ended. Under Henry and his son, Henry VIII, there was a change in the defensive policies of the realm. Both kings started building a fleet of ships owned by the Crown instead of simply impressing merchantmen in time of war. Both, too, built fortresses and batteries to protect the coast. Harwich was fortified in this period, and the first fort was built over the Orwell estuary at Landguard Point. Harwich always regarded this as part of its own defences, and the County of Essex claimed responsibility for it, even though it was on the Suffolk shore. Landguard is still occupied by the army today, though it has been completely rebuilt since Tudor days. Another fort was raised on Mersea Island at the mouth of the Colne. This, which has almost completely disappeared now, was triangular in shape, about one hundred yards long on each side, mounting cannon on the walls. A third fort, still standing but much changed, is at Tilbury in Essex, guarding the Thames.

Kett's rebellion

In 1549, during the reign of Edward VI, a serious rebellion broke out in Norfolk, led by a local gentleman named Kett. The grievance of the rebels was the loss of common grazing land as the countryside was enclosed by hedges. After sacking Wymondham, the rebels first encamped on Mousehold Heath, outside Norwich, and then stormed the city by the Bishop's Bridge. The rebellion became more serious when twelve hundred Crown troops, including Italian mercenaries, were defeated. The government took no chances on there being a second defeat, and sent twelve thousand men to the attack some weeks later. The battle was fought on St Andrew's Plain, Norwich, and the rebels were routed.

The Spanish Armada

Elizabeth's reign, from an East Anglian military point of view, is the story of the Spanish Armada of 1588. The previous year the 'Queen's General' had made a tour of inspection in East Anglia, and had found preparations woefully inadequate. Landguard, for instance, was completely indefensible. It stood on a shore so steep that enemy galleons could approach close enough for landing parties to jump ashore. Earthworks were raised on the cliffs between Lowestoft and Gorleston, and a battery of twenty guns was raised at Aldeburgh. Southwold too had its battery on modern Gun Hill, though the cannons to be seen there today were not given to the town until 1746, when the Duke of Cumberland stopped in the harbour on his way to Culloden.

In March 1588, an order was made to the effect that the East Anglian coastal towns were to furnish ships for the Queen's service. Ipswich and Harwich, for instance, were linked, and their joint contribution was assessed at two ships and a pinnace. Without exception, the coastal towns protested that trade was poor, and that they simply could not afford to send the ships which had been asked for. Even when they did send vessels, all too often these were of inferior quality. The *Matthew*, Lowestoft's ship, was dismissed as being 'not worth keeping', while Aldeburgh sent the *Marygold* without any provisions, and this vessel too was not kept.

The main camp of the army was at Tilbury, and the remains of the earthworks can still be seen near the church at West Tilbury. In the early days of August 1588, the Earl of Leicester laboured to get the site into something resembling a military camp. He was short of everything, including men. Two thousand Suffolk men had been ordered to report there by 9 August, as had three thousand Norfolk militia. The problem was that the counties were not happy about letting their defenders outside the

Queen Elizabeth reviewing her
troops at Tilbury. It was in her
famous address to the troops on
that occasion that she said that
although she had the body of a
woman she had the spirit of a ruler
of England.

Great Yarmouth. A plan of Queen Elizabeth's
time, in the Cottonian Collection. It shows the
town defences typical of many coast towns in
the reigns of Henry VIII and Elizabeth I.
Unfortunately, all too often the defences were
in a ruinous condition.

county boundaries. Norfolk, in fact, demanded assurances from the Privy Council that Norfolk would not be left undefended, and the Council had to promise that in the event of invasion other counties' militia would be sent. Even the Essex militia was late. When the four thousand eventually did arrive, they were full of spirit. Finding nothing to eat, they remarked that they were prepared to abide worse hunger in the service of the Queen.

They saw the Queen on 18 August. She came by barge from London and landed at Tilbury Fort, observing the bridge of boats that was being pre-pared to enable the army to cross to the south of the Thames if necessary. Then she rode among the troops without escort, bareheaded, and wearing a silver cuirass over her white velvet dress. The troops cheered her to the echo as she told them, 'I myself will be your General.'

Soon the Armada was sighted off Harwich, but it had been broken by Drake and the other Captains and was in flight. The camp at Tilbury broke up, and peace descended for fifty years, until king and Parliament began the constitutional disputes that were to lead to Civil War.

6

THE CIVIL WAR

THROUGHOUT the summer of 1642, both king and Parliament were preparing for the inevitable struggle. East Anglia generally was for Parliament, Suffolk particularly being firm in its support. Towns like Ipswich had great numbers of Puritans, many of whom held positions of responsibility and influence in local affairs. Among the pre-hostility manoeuvring which took place in Suffolk was the movement to ensure that the key to the county magazine at Bury was held by 'trustworthy' (i.e. Parliamentary) people. Also the lists of those liable to militia service, held at Stowmarket, were kept in the right hands.

There were a few exceptions to the support for Parliament. The Cambridge Colleges were with the king, and attempted to send money for the royalist cause. The whole of the University plate was to be sent. Such a move had been foreseen by a young Huntingdonshire squire who was to find fame and a place in history. His name was Oliver Cromwell. Not only did he intercept the plate, but also had a guard put on the bridges out of Cambridge to keep a watch for the king's agents. As part of this scheme the old earthworks that had formed William the Conqueror's castle were used as a strongpoint.

The Eastern association

With the Battle of Edgehill, in October 1642, the conflict became open, and the two sides struggled to raise armies. Two months later, the Eastern Association was formed. This was the banding together of the counties of Norfolk, Suffolk, Essex, Cambridgeshire and Hertfordshire. The motive for this was the mutual protection of the member counties. There was a great deal of selfishness among the county leaders of this time, who thought more in terms of keeping the war out of their own areas than taking part in any nationwide operations. Strength lay in unity, so the Eastern Association

was formed among those counties which were felt to have the same long-term interests. The Association was run by a committee that met at Cambridge. In addition, each county also had a committee, usually of country gentlemen, to see to the county affairs. The armed forces that were raised by the Association were placed under the command of the well-liked Earl of Manchester.

So began 1643. All over the Eastern counties men were being recruited and trained. Cromwell was there raising cavalry. One troop was raised from public subscription at Norwich, and became known as the 'Maidens' Troop' because the story grew up that the troop had been raised from money given by young women as a kind of protest against the royalists' alleged habit of ravishing any young women that fell into their hands. The county committees were busy raising horses – always a vital commodity in wars of these times – by buying, borrowing, or requisitioning them. Wains and carts were requisitioned from the country folk and pressed into service to take arms and ammunition to Cambridge, which acted as a kind of forward supply base to the Parliamentary field armies. All those who volunteered to serve outside the territory of the Association were billeted at many of our East Anglian inns – inns like the 'Cross Keys', 'Wrestlers' and 'Wild Man' at Bury – before being transported across the Ouse and the Cam by the watermen, who were doing rather well out of the extra business that war had brought them. Ipswich, in the meantime, was preparing to defend itself. Two men had been sent to Colchester to ask the military engineer there to come up to Ipswich. In addition the town treasurer was ordered to buy sixty wheelbarrows to be used to aid the construction of breastworks and palisades around the town.

The siege of King's Lynn

It was amid all this activity that the town of Lynn declared for the king, and ever since has been called King's Lynn. The trouble arose in August 1643 when Sir Haman Le Strange gained the upper hand on the town council. Le Strange had extracted a promise from the king that he would relieve Lynn if it was besieged, and this was all Le Strange needed to close the gates of the town to Parliament.

The first troops sent to investigate were Captain Poe's company of Essex militia. They were met by a severe hail of musketry as they approached, and retreated to report on what Poe had seen. Lynn was

strong in arms: there were no less than forty cannon in the place, together with twelve hundred muskets and five hundred barrels of powder. For all that Poe believed that the place would be taken in five days, if only the besieged were not reinforced from the sea.

The besieging army under the Earl of Manchester was on its way. Gathering a force of 1,500 foot and twice as many horse, he arrived and threw a blockade round the landward side of the town. At the same time, the Earl of Warwick arrived with a Parliamentary squadron to blockade the sea entrance to Lynn. The city of Norwich lent its ordnance, including the heavy old demi-culverin (which weighed over two tons) and the lighter falconets.

There was some discussion among the besiegers as to whether to storm the town or starve it out. Among those in favour of assault was Cromwell, and

Part of the walls of King's Lynn today. See also the watercolour of the East Gate. The town was entirely fortified but it was the lack of help from outside which doomed the garrison.

his party carried the day. The old town of Lynn was stormed without too much opposition, and was guarded by the Roundhead pickets. The old town formed a good place for the artillery to be sited to command the rest of the town. Batteries were quickly raised to command the South Causeway and the East Gate as well as the moated side of the town. The town still resisted fiercely, and the ensuing bombardment did much damage. On 3 September the church of St Margaret was struck by an 18-pound ball while a service was in progress. That ball is still preserved today at nearby Union Court.

The date set for the assault was the Saturday a fortnight after this. The besiegers were preparing boats for a waterborne attack, and cartloads of storming ladders were brought up ready. The cannonading was furious, and about eighty on each side were killed and wounded. Suddenly, terms were asked for, and a Parliamentary deputation went through the lines to parley. This did not prevent the besieged from continuing to strengthen their defences. Some of them were felling trees to make obstacles, while another party attempted to

The East Gate, King's Lynn (from a watercolour by Rev. Edward Edwards). The loss of the Old Town led to the Roundheads being able to mount a heavy bombardment of this gate.

break the banks on some dykes so as to flood the ground over which the attackers would have to advance. Seven of these townsmen were captured and slain, and their naked bodies placed near one of the town gates. This weakened the resolve of the besieged, and their resistance finally collapsed when the Parliamentary army paraded in full strength, flags flying and drums beating, within sight of the walls. The town surrendered on 19 September.

The New Model Army

In 1644, East Anglia was the only area which was really secure for Parliament. Elsewhere, there were local struggles between royalists and Roundheads. The Eastern Association saw the war as being simply a matter of defending East Anglia, and were unwilling to lend troops for other projects. During

Waller's advance on Oxford in 1644, three thousand Suffolk men were sent to guard the north flank of the army. These men all displayed a great lack of enthusiasm, and were anxious to return home to get in the harvest. After Waller's defeat at Cropredy, they were compelled to remain under arms until the victory at Marston Moor altered the situation in Parliament's favour.

It was incidents like this which led Cromwell to see the need for a professional army, regularly paid by Parliament and not subject to restrictions as to the area in which it would operate. This army would be a 'New Model' for military forces. In January 1645, a conference met at Bury to discuss the formation of the New Model Army. Naturally, the East Anglian County Committees were opposed to the idea on the grounds that an offensive war was not in the spirit of the underlying idea of the Association, i.e. mutual defence. Also, each county wished to retain the authority to raise and pay its own men. The passing of the New Model Ordinance by Parliament left them no choice in the matter, and East Anglia contributed four regiments of foot and a great deal of cavalry to the new force. It was from East Anglia that the archetypal hymn-singing 'Ironside' trooper originated. At the same time, Cromwell was appointed Commander-in-Chief of the forces of the Association, and sat on the committee at Cambridge.

Three years later, in 1648, even Puritan towns like Ipswich were ready to welcome the return of the king, who was a prisoner of Parliament. What really frightened them was the prospect of military government. This was further exacerbated by the fact that numbers of New Model officers had sprung from the ranks of 'such as have filled dung carts', which did not endear them to many of the county gentlemen. The result was a series of riots across the region. At Norwich, for instance, a riot broke out when the mob resisted an officer sent to take the royalist mayor to London. The city gates were shut against Fleetwood's Horse Regiment, and a potential rising averted only when the rioters' magazine (on the site of Bethlehem Hospital) blew up. This was at the end of April. A week later there was a riot at Bury, when a mob 'ran horribly mad upon a Maypole'. On 4 May, the people of Essex presented a petition of 30,000 names to Parliament begging for peace with the king.

Royalist risings

With the country enjoying a widespread revival of royalist feeling, the time seemed ripe for a royalist counter-revolution. There were large numbers of men who had fought in the king's forces and who had returned home defeated. These were all awaiting the signal to rise. What made this dangerous situation even worse was the fact that both Wales and Scotland were in arms against Parliament. General 'Black Tom' Fairfax was preparing to go north to stop the Scots invasion, and his departure would leave the south-east defenceless.

Tilbury Fort where the Parliamentary Army landed from south of the Thames and from which the Colchester campaign was launched.

A group of plotters in Kent were waiting for this before striking. They knew that a rebellion would only stand a chance if it were not opposed in the early days. Unfortunately for them, events were moving so swiftly that they could not be controlled. A petition, similar to the one presented to Parliament by the people of Essex, was drawn up by the Kentish folk. The County Committee tried to repress it, and somehow the word got about that two petitioners from every borough would be hanged. The final spark to the powder keg was the arrival at Sandwich of an impostor who claimed to be the Prince of Wales.

The whole county rose in revolt on 21 May. The next day the local gentry, seeing the depth of feeling, agreed to lead the revolt. The crews of six naval ships in the Downs also joined in, and the plan was for the rebels to gather on Blackheath, just outside London, where a bridge of boats was to be flung across the Thames so that the Essex men could join the Kentish rebels.

The feeling in the Army was one of derision, most being of the opinion that the whole business would be over once the rebels got a glimpse of Parliamentary cavalry. General Fairfax delayed his departure for Scotland and pushed down into Kent, and he found the rebels waiting for him outside Maidstone on 1 June 1648. The rebels were led by the Earl of Norwich. They had elected the Earl of Holland to lead them, but Norwich had turned up with a blank commission from the Prince of Wales, into which he had entered his own name, and thus claimed the command as his right.

By midnight the rebels had been shattered. Maidstone was back in Parliamentary hands, and Norwich was running north-east with about 3,000 men. He was heading towards London, hoping to find support there, and reached Blackheath on 3 June. Fairfax was involved with the pacification of Kent, and sent Colonel Edmund Whalley's dragoons in pursuit of Norwich. Norwich found that the gates of London were closed against him. With Whalley closing in from behind, there was only one route open to him. He had heard that Essex was ripe for a rising. That night, he crossed the Thames alone to ride up to Chelmsford to gather intelligence for himself. His followers panicked in his absence and dispersed; most went to Surrey, and only some five hundred crossed the river in boats to the Essex side. Norwich returned in the morning, having found no trace of rebellion in Essex. His force seized Bow Bridge, which today is in central London, but which then was the communicating bridge between Essex and the City. Norwich hoped that he would be able to hold it until Essex rose, but that night he received information that Whalley's trained cavalry had crossed London Bridge and were in the Mile End Road. In the face of this, Norwich decided to retreat.

Meanwhile, royalist feeling was beginning to make itself felt in Essex. That same day, 4 June, the County Committee met at Chelmsford to discuss the best way of dealing with the royalist threat. The whole Committee was arrested by the mob, led by a certain Colonel Farr. This so worried Parliament that they passed an Ordinance of Indemnity, pardoning all Essex men who had taken part in the rioting. The only proviso was that Norwich's men were not to be harboured or comforted. It seemed that most people were inclined to accept this condition, judging by the reception the Act received when it was read out at Chelmsford on the 6th.

In a desperate effort to prevent the acceptance of this condition, Norwich left his forces again and came to Chelmsford on the 7th. There he found Sir Charles Lucas, a native Essex man, who held the king's commission to lead the county. Lucas addressed the mob so persuasively on Norwich's behalf that a great number of the militia remained in arms and were willing to fight for the royalist side. Norwich returned to get his men, and the two forces met at Brentwood on the 8th.

The next day, Chelmsford was occupied by the combined force. They faced a problem almost at once. Sir Thomas Honeywood, a member of the County Committee, had been absent from the last meeting, and had thus escaped the arrest of the members. He had raised the militia of the northern part of the county, and had gathered them around his own house, Mark's Hall near Coggeshall. He had 1,200 men there, and was waiting for Whalley's Horse to come up and join him. In the meantime, Honeywood raided the county magazine at Braintree and took off what he could.

This was a blow to the Royalists, many of whom were unarmed, who were marching on Braintree. This setback was made up to some extent by a raid on Lord Warwick's house at Leighs, where they found five hundred stand of arms. They reached Braintree on the tenth, and spent two days trying to organize themselves and decide what to do next. Norwich believed that arms and ammunition would be delivered to him from friends of the king on the Continent, and wanted to push farther into Essex to the Suffolk border. Lucas, who was a Colchester man, believed that he was so well-liked in his home-town that recruits would flock to the cause. It was his advice which was eventually taken on the plan of action.

The problem was that Coggeshall, where Honeywood was, lay between them and Colchester. Whalley was behind them, though in fact he was keeping his distance. He thought that the countryside, with its thick hedgerows, was ideal for ambushes of horsemen by foot soldiers, as the cavalry would not have room to deploy. The royalists set out from Braintree that night, moving north-west as if going towards Cambridge. This was a ruse; they counter-marched to Braintree, rested for a while, then struck out again, this time north-east. They marched as far as Halstead, then struck straight for Colchester, having successfully avoided Coggeshall and Honeywood's men. The next morning, they were admitted into the town of Colchester. Some attempt was made to resist their entry, but the royalist party in the town prevailed.

If they had expected to gather recruits and then

The Siege House, Colchester, held as an outpost by the Royalists. It fell to the attack of the Suffolk Trained Bands. Bullet holes may still be seen in the walls.

continue, they were mistaken. Fairfax himself was ready to take the field against them, having pacified Kent. On Sunday, 11 June, he was at Gravesend, where he heard morning service. After that, he crossed the Thames to Tilbury with all the troops he could muster. Many of the troopers must have taken advantage of the Old Forge, which still stands facing the green, to have their mounts shoed. Others stabled their horses in the nave of the church. Fairfax, though racked with gout, pushed on to Billericay, impatient to know whether Honeywood had managed to stop the rebels. With his horsemen exhausted, he still could not curb his impatience, and rode on again with ten companions, leaving his forces at Billericay. By next morning, 12 June, he was within ten miles of Coggeshall, where he met Honeywood and Whalley, who had discovered by then that the royalists had slipped by them.

Tireless, Fairfax took the thousand men of Whalley's Regiment and pushed on towards Colchester. That evening, he was a mere mile away, at Lexden. On the 13th, he was joined by the rest of his cavalry. At noon that day, a great cloud of dust marked the line of march of a column which turned out to be his infantry brigade, led by Colonel Berkstead. There must have been some surprise in Fairfax's camp as these veterans staggered in; they had marched from Tilbury up to Lexden, a distance of over fifty miles, in forty-eight hours. The arrival of these men gave Fairfax a force of five thousand veterans to throw against four thousand royalists, only half of whom were armed.

Lucas, being a more experienced soldier than Norwich, had taken over executive command of the royalist forces. A search of Colchester had produced seventy barrels of powder and a thousand weapons had been found in private houses. Lucas resolved to make a stand, and on the 13th, while Fairfax's infantry was coming up, the royalists drew up outside the town to await attack. Lucas had chosen his ground well. Colchester was not an easy place to defend. The royalists were trying to hold the line of the old Roman walls. These were incomplete and there were only two bastions to provide flanking fire on the whole wall. Fairfax's army, which was coming up the London Road, was nevertheless at a disadvantage. The road came up to the south-west angle of the town walls, and then ran along the foot of the south wall for a little way before entering the town through the Head Gate. The establishment of a battery in the churchyard of St Mary's, which lay right at the south-west corner, meant that Fairfax would have to advance in the face of cannon fire. Also on this south face, the ground fell away just outside the walls, and rose again at some distance. On the higher ground stood a number of buildings suitable for outposts, such as St John's Abbey and Lucas's own house.

Lucas drew up his men across the London Road. In the middle stood the foot, while the scanty amount of cavalry held the wings. The right was protected by the nature of the ground, which dropped away steeply towards the Colne. The left flank of the infantry was protected by the thick hedges that ran along the sides of the Maldon Road, though the cavalry, who were on the other side of the hedges, had no cover at all.

It was in Fairfax's interests to take the town quickly, as events in Scotland were pressing and he could not afford to be tied up in Essex for long. Hoping to win another victory like Maidstone, he simply ordered Berkstead's infantry forward to carry the town with a rush. To Fairfax's amazement, these veterans were stopped and flung back by some very steady royalist musketry. Twice more this happened. On the royalist left, the Roundheads were having more success. Fairfax had committed his cavalry, and these were so superior in numbers that they quickly routed the royalist horse. Having done so, they sought to imitate Cromwell's tactics at Naseby and take the royalist line in flank, rolling it up. It was here that they came unstuck, for the thick hedgerows along the Maldon Road were lined with pikemen and musketeers. It was an impenetrable barrier. Still, the Roundhead cavalry pressed

its attack, so that Lucas was forced to send more infantry to strengthen the flank. This in turn left the centre dangerously weak and, seeing Berkstead's infantry preparing to come on again, Lucas ordered a withdrawal inside the walls. Berkstead saw the retreat, and pressed forward. About four hundred of the royalists were dead or wounded, and Berkstead assumed that the royalist army was routed. When he saw that nobody had closed the Head Gate behind the royalists, he decided to enter the town and take it by storm.

As soon as the leading ranks were inside the gate, they realized that they had walked into a trap. Just inside the gate, the street rises. At the top were a body of cavalry who charged irresistibly, having the advantage of both the terrain and surprise. At the same time, a company of foot charged from a lane that led to St Mary's, taking the Roundheads in flank, and bundling them out of the gate again. As the gates swung shut, Lucas came and fastened the bar, for want of a better peg, with the cane that he carried in his hand. Though Fairfax's troops made several more attacks, it soon became clear that a siege was going to be inevitable.

The next day, the besieged were busy at work strengthening their defences, 'like the Jews in Jerusalem, with our swords in one hand and our trowels in the other, we began to repair the ruines of our walls.' Fairfax, too, was not idle. He felt that his first task was to cut the town off from any hope of relief by sea, and he sent a troop of dragoons to secure the fort on Mersea Island which commanded the mouth of the Colne. They took it without trouble, but were only just in time. The royalists, suddenly aware of the importance of the place, sent out a force of mounted men, who arrived too late. They did not venture to dispute ownership of the strongpoint with the dragoons, and retired to Colchester.

The remains of the fort, though disappointing, may still be seen today. Take the road towards East Mersea and stop at the place where the bus turns round. Walk down to the sea wall, turn right, and a few hundred yards away you will see a blockhouse of the Second World War. The fort lies about fifty yards away from here, and appears as two grassy embankments, each fifty yards long. Where they join is the site of the old seaward turret. Even these remains will probably be encroached on in a few years by the sea.

Fairfax was casting a net around Colchester, but he still feared that the mounted royalists could make their escape towards the north. He posted strong bodies of troops in this direction, and sent urgent appeals for the County authorities of Suffolk to send their trained bands down to the siege. At this point, Fairfax's attention was diverted by events in his rear. Newmarket had always been a centre of anti-Parliamentary feeling since the troubles began. On the thirteenth, when the two armies were fighting outside the walls of Colchester, a number of men from the Newmarket area gathered in the royalist cause. They were led by Captain John Appleyard of Dullingham, and numbered five hundred. Intending to take part in the relief of the royalists in Colchester, they moved down to Linton, which lies on the Cambridge–Essex border. While they were at Linton, on the night of 16 June, they were attacked in the dark by the troops of Captain Robert Sparrow of Wickhambrook, who utterly defeated them.

The royalists suffered an even greater setback as the result of this incident. Suffolk was wavering in its loyalty, unsure whether to intervene or not. The arrival of Appleyard's rebels at Linton, which is right on the Suffolk border, seems to have filled the Suffolk authorities with apprehension that the county might be invaded by marauding royalists.

On 17 June, therefore, Ipswich Corporation decided that its militia should be sent down to Cattawade Bridge (just outside Manningtree) to prevent the royalists breaking into the county of Suffolk. This at least was something, though Fairfax had hoped to have Suffolk men in the siege lines.

On 19 June, the Roundheads also won another success. Three vessels laden with supplies for the besieged attempted to run up the Colne. Two Roundhead vessels from Harwich were waiting in Brightlingsea Creek, and swooped out. Caught between them and the guns of Mersea Fort, the royalists were compelled to surrender. The firing could be heard in Colchester, and Norwich sent a party of cavalry out to intervene if possible. They were too late, and retreated without taking part in the action.

With the double-blow of this and the incident at Linton, Fairfax felt strong enough to ask for the

Helmet of the Royalist leader Sir Charles Lucas, dogged defender of Colchester during the siege. He was a local knight and was executed in the grounds of the castle.

town to surrender. As was the custom, the message was taken by a trumpeter. Not only did Norwich refuse to surrender, but also enquired after the state of Fairfax's gout. When the trumpeter replied that Fairfax was still suffering, Norwich promised that the royalists would soon cure it for Fairfax by giving him something far worse to worry about. With this refusal, Fairfax settled down to take Colchester by a siege that he knew would be long and bitter.

Already he had constructed a number of forts around Colchester. On the south, there were a number of strongpoints, such as fort Needham and the Berkstead fort, which cut off Colchester from the south. The northern exits were still a source of worry. On 24 June, Fairfax won another political success when he managed to persuade the Suffolk authorities that the interests of Suffolk would be served best by the Suffolk militia taking a more active part in the siege. They came marching into Essex to join in, a valuable reinforcement and one which helped to block the escape route north.

The royalists were holding the church at East Grinstead as an outpost. On 29 June, the Suffolk men, with a stiffening of veterans from Ingoldsby's Regiment, assaulted and took the church after a very bloody skirmish. They raised earthworks there to command the Suffolk road. A forward battery was erected right at the end of the bridge over the Colne that linked Colchester with the Suffolk road. On the Colchester side of the river, the Roundhead earthworks were gradually extended until they also reached the bridge.

By 2 July, the ring of earthworks was complete. A glance at the map shows how Colchester, which lies in a bend of the Colne, was surrounded by earthworks of which both ends also lay on the river, while the north bank generally, and the exits of the two bridges particularly, were guarded by numbers of detached works.

The assault was to be made from the south, with the besiegers gradually working forward by bombarding strongpoints, assaulting them, refortifying them and erecting batteries so as to start the whole process all over again on the next target. It was during this phase of the operations that the besiegers began to become embittered. The reason for this was that they were convinced that the royalists were using poisoned bullets, or roughened ones

Opposite Massive ruins of St Botolph's Priory, off one of the main streets of Colchester. The Priory was damaged during the siege when the Roundheads bombarded it in an attempt to take the Priory and use it as a forward assault base.

which caused worse wounds than the normal musket balls. One of these is in the Castle Museum; probably the roughness was due more to a lack of casting facilities than an intention to commit atrocities.

At any rate, Fairfax gradually worked closer. On 14 July, he seized Lucas's house and the Hythe, the landing place of boats from Colne Mouth. The next day, the cannon were at work against the Abbey of St John of Giles. The Abbey, built soon after the Norman Conquest, was in ruins; all that stood was the later fourteenth-century gatehouse. This was a vital position, as it commanded the whole of the south wall of the town. It fell to storm that same day; the marks of the cannon balls can still be seen on the gatehouse today. From here, the next point of assault was the great Norman church of St Botolph's. A battery placed in front of the church of St Mary Magdelene soon ruined its massive walls. If you use the Priory Street car park today, and walk towards the town centre, you pass these ruins; there are few more impressive in their size and utter silence.

Lucas was doing all that he could. There were constant sallies, and the Suffolk men were engaged in a particularly bloody one on a dark Tuesday night. This took place outside the east gate, in East Street. One link with the fighting here is the Old Siege House, which can be seen today. It is riddled with bullet holes, a number of which have been circled with red paint.

For all their courage, the royalists were lost. By the beginning of August, famine was rampant in Colchester. The civilian population fared worst, as the fighting men had first share of what food there was. Very quickly the citizens of Colchester lost their enthusiasm for the royalist cause, and the royalist leaders were faced with the task not only of defending the town against the Roundheads but also of holding a hostile population in check. The mayor wrote to Fairfax, begging him to allow the civilians out. Fairfax quite naturally refused; the civilians were eating up the defenders' food supplies.

On 17 August, the royalists offered to surrender in twenty days if they had not been relieved in that time. Fairfax refused these terms, as he said that he intended to take the town by storm within the royalists' time-limit. As a further move to intimidate the town, he actually had the paraphernalia for an assault brought up to where the besieged could see it.

By now, Norwich was having the greatest difficulty in keeping the populace in check. On one occasion, he was surrounded by starving women who begged for food or the surrender of the town. Norwich brutally told them that he would see them eat their children before he would surrender. Despite this boast, he asked Fairfax for terms the next day. Fairfax gave his answer on 20 August: all soldiers under the rank of Captain could go free, all above would have to surrender at mercy. Norwich refused these terms, and the siege went on. Then, on 22 August, Fairfax heard that Cromwell had beaten the invading Scots at Preston. Now there was no reason for him to go to the North, he could devote as much time and energy to the siege as was needed. He made sure that the garrison heard the news, and had proclamations shot into the town, telling them that there was no longer any military reason to hang on. The royalists realized that nothing could save them, and resolved to make an attempt to break through the lines on the night of 25 August. Those who still had horses, mostly nobles and gentlemen, were eager for this. Not so the common foot-soldiers, who thought that they would be abandoned to their fate once the party got outside the walls. They therefore refused to take part, and also threatened to shoot down any horse-man who attempted to escape.

Next morning, they decided that they had had enough. If Norwich did not surrender the town, they would arrest the officers and take them to Fairfax. In the face of this, Norwich sent delegates that same day to discuss surrender. The terms were harsher now; the privates had only their lives guaranteed, the officers had nothing. They were to ask for mercy, and there was no guarantee that they would not be killed anyway.

On 28 August, the town was occupied, and a council met to decide which royalists were to die. Norwich was not killed, but Lucas and another professional soldier named Lisle were sentenced to death. At 7 p.m. that night, they were led into the grassy yard on the south side of Colchester Castle. Lisle was shot first, and Lucas caught him and kissed him before going in front of the firing squad himself. He called the executioners closer, and one of them called out, 'I warrant we'll hit you, sir.' Recalling the desperate sorties of the siege, Lucas smiled and replied, 'I've been closer than this and you have missed me.' This time the musketeers did not miss, and today there is an obelisk in Castle Park on the spot where the two men are said to have died.

The other gentlemen were held to ransom, while the common soldiers were first imprisoned in various churches, then marched to Bristol. There they were loaded aboard ships bound for the West Indies, to spend the rest of their lives as slaves on the sugar plantations. The town itself was fined £14,000, which Fairfax had promised his soldiers in lieu of the plunder which they would have had if the town had been stormed.

7

THE DUTCH WARS

It is an interesting though surprising fact that London in latitude is actually south of Amsterdam. Also, both of the nations engaged in the Dutch Wars border on the North Sea. These two facts account for the importance of East Anglia's coastline in the series of conflicts between England and Holland that were to last through the latter half of the seventeenth century.

The immediate cause of the wars was trade: the growing commercial rivalry between England and Holland in the carrying trade was the most important bone of contention. The Dutch feared that the English control of the Straits of Dover meant that their trade routes could be closed at will by England. There was also a problem over disputed fishing grounds, particularly in the North Sea herring industry.

The battle of Lowestoft

The First Dutch War was fought by the Commonwealth over the period 1651–4. It was a popular war, and one in which England did well, winning one battle off Dover and another off the Kentish Knock. The war decided nothing, and hostilities flared up again just after the Restoration in 1660. At first the incidents were confined to privateers raiding merchant shipping. Then, on 14 January 1665 the Dutch declared war. At once there was a scramble to prepare the fleets for sea. The English were ready first, and sent 109 assorted men-o'-war under James, Duke of York (later King James II) to cruise off the Texel. The strategy behind this was the interception of the Dutch homeward-bound convoys, a rich prize indeed.

Then, for the first time, the corrupt administration that was to hamstring the English navy's effectiveness throughout these wars reared its head. James's fleet was so badly equipped with essential supplies that he was unable to keep his station, and

put back into Harwich. The supply situation was further aggravated on 20 May when the Dutch fleet, which had left harbour to cruise the North Sea, snapped up ten merchantmen laden with very valuable naval material. So serious was this loss that the English fleet was hurried to sea again. It had been lying off the Gunfleet – a sandbank that lies just off the Essex coast opposite Dovercourt – and weighed anchor on 29 May.

That night, as it lay off Aldeburgh, Suffolk, James received news that the Dutch were near. Sailing on through the night, he dropped anchor in Southwold Bay (a name usually shortened to 'Solebay'). The visitor to Southwold might be surprised to hear of the importance of Southwold during the Dutch Wars. Today Southwold is a pleasant seaside resort, its only link with the past being the seven cannons preserved on Gun Hill, itself the site of the old battery. In fact, it has been the action of the sea, scouring away at the coastline, that has eradicated the main reason for Southwold's popularity with the English fleet. For where the coast now runs almost straight north–south, there was three hundred years ago a wide bay; large enough to accommodate the whole fleet from the sudden storms that howl from the east and which have pushed so many sailing ships to destruction on a lee shore. In addition, Southwold had fine clear freshwater springs which were popular with our admirals.

James was still in the bay at midday when a frigate brought back the news that the Dutch were no more than six miles east-south-east of the English. Though James weighed anchor at once, it was to be four days before battle was joined. The Dutch Admiral Obdam was worried about the

Overleaf Dramatic climax of the sea battle off Lowestoft, 13 June 1665, when the Dutch flagship of Admiral Obdam blew up and sank with all hands (bottom left corner of the print).

Abbildung der Mächtigen Seeschlacht, so sich zwischen ...
Juny. Anno 1665. zugetragen, darin ...

IHRE HOCHHEIT, HERTZOG VON YORCK OBERSTER ADMIRAL.

A. Hertzog von Yorck. B. ...
Samson: D. der Vice Admir...
vnd Schmidt, F. Admiral Op...
G. Iohan Eberts. H. Corde...
tain Hahn. L. das Schiff Me...

Engeland.

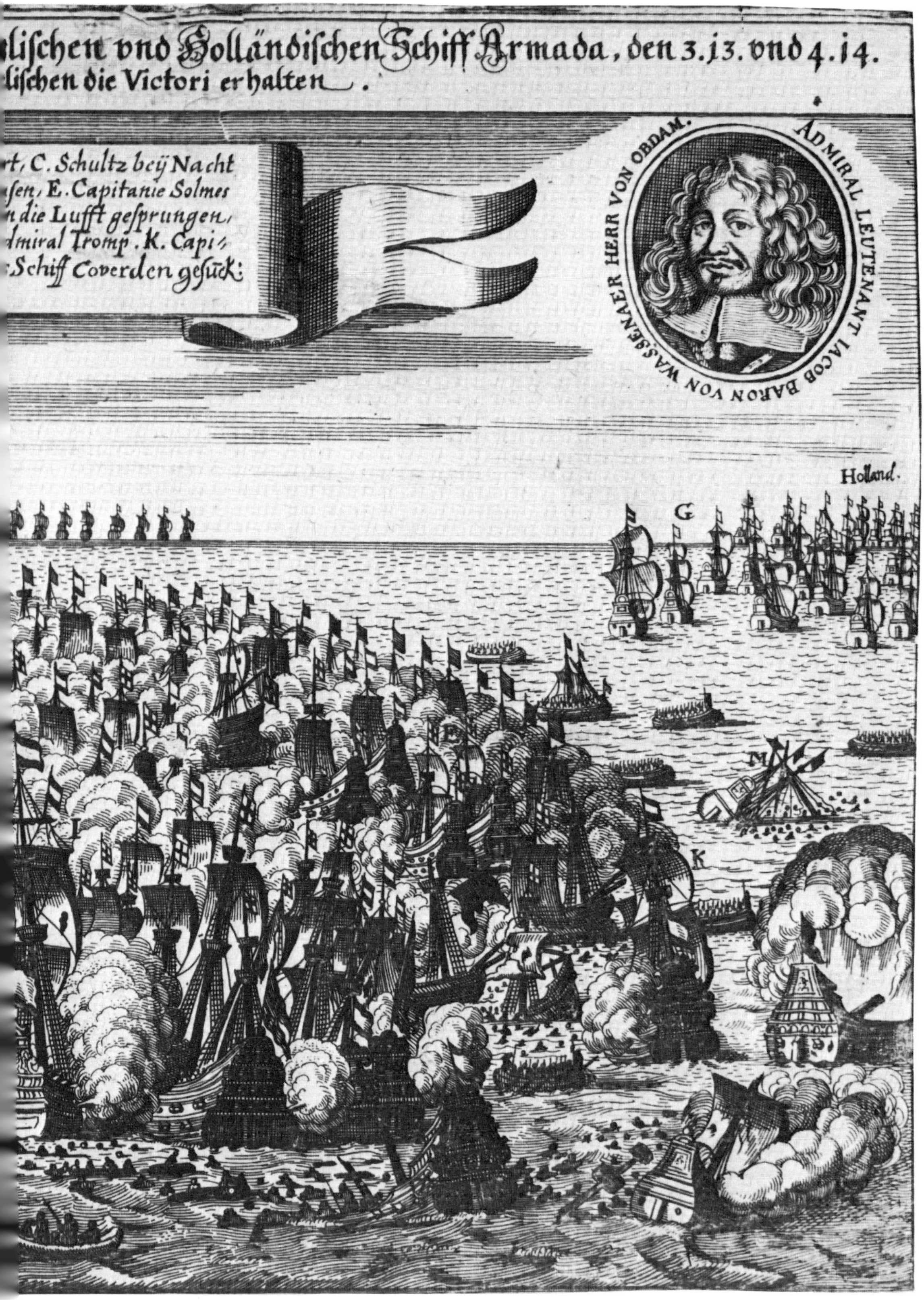

rt, C. Schultz beÿ Nacht
sen. E. Capitanie Solmes
n die Lufft gesprungen,
dmiral Tromp. K. Capi-
s Schiff Coverden gesuck:

ADMIRAL LEUTENANT IACOB BARON VON WASSENAER HERR VON OBDAM.

Holland.

G

E

M

K

condition of his fleet. Not only was there a lack of discipline, but bickering had broken out among the officers. In addition, some of the ships were quite unseaworthy, and others of the fleet were dispersed for miles. Despite this, Obdam was attempting to obey his orders to press the English coast when James came out. Obdam had to avoid action until his fleet could concentrate. For the next few days both fleets manoeuvred in sight of the Suffolk coast, until, on 3 June, the engagement began at 2.30 a.m. just north-east of Lowestoft.

With the wind in the south-west, the English had the weather gauge – an important tactical advantage because it meant that they could give or avoid action as they wished. The English formed line, with Prince Rupert in the van, James in the centre, and the Earl of Sandwich in the rear. The two lines passed, exchanging broadsides, then tacked round to renew the fight. At about 1 p.m., Sandwich's squadron got badly entangled with the Dutch centre. Somehow, the English squadron managed to pass right through the Dutch fleet, cutting it into two parts. Now all order was gone and a tangled mêlée ensued. Obdam's ship, *Eendracht*, came alongside James's flagship, *Royal Charles*, and poured such a fire into it that the English were in danger of sinking. A single shot killed Lord Muskerry, the Earl of Falmouth and the Earl of Burlington's son. James was drenched by their blood and cut in the hand by a flying splinter of skull. Suddenly, there was a great rumbling explosion and the *Eendracht* blew up. Some loose powder had been touched off and this had ignited the main magazine. Within moments the ship was beneath the waves, taking all four hundred souls aboard with her.

The loss of the flagship was the turning point in the battle. While a few of the Dutch ships continued the battle, the great majority put up their helms and ran before the wind for safety. Even in retreat the Dutch were in confusion. Command had devolved on to Jan Evertsen, who set course for the Maas. For some reason Cornelius van Tromp thought that *he* was in command; and he led as much of the fleet as he could back towards the Texel. The final blow to the Dutch came when four of their ships ran foul of each other and were all set afire by a single English fireship. So ended the Battle of Lowestoft. The Dutch had lost a total of thirty-two ships, the English had lost two. It might have been a more complete victory had the English pursued. They did not, despite their light losses, and returned to Southwold.

The St James's Day battle

Next year, 1666, the Dutch were joined by the French. Prince Rupert was in command of the English fleet, and was badly beaten in the 'Four Days Fight' in the Channel. Despite this, the fleet was refitted and was back at the anchorage at the Gunfleet off Harwich on 22 July when the news was received that the enemy were only eighteen miles to the north-east. Rupert at once weighed anchor, and there followed the usual duelling for the weather gauge. It must have been a magnificent sight. A contemporary account tells us that the whole sea area from the Thames estuary to Orfordness in Suffolk was filled with the splendid ships of the line under great clouds of canvas. In the early morning of 25 July, St James's Day, the wind was from the north, and the Dutch were to the north-east of the English at the Gunfleet. The Dutch line was almost six miles long, and it was extremely ill-formed. There was a very dangerous gap between the centre and the rear, which was commanded by Cornelius van Tromp.

The van and centre had been brought to action, and the English rear was clawing up to engage Van Tromp when the most extraordinary thing happened. Van Tromp simply started to run southwards, broke round the English rearmost ships, and headed west towards the coast of East Anglia. This move completely separated him from his friends, who were south-east, and left the full English fleet between them. The Dutch commander, Admiral de Ruyter, was completely mystified by his subordinate's behaviour. He later complained bitterly to his government about Van Tromp. Meanwhile, the rear and centre were being pounded hard by the English, heading almost due east away from Van Tromp. In the van, the English soon established their superiority, though in the centre the fight was more equal and both sides displayed incredible determination. By four in the afternoon the Dutch were beaten, drifting south, too exhausted to fight any longer. The English made one attempt to re-engage as night was falling, but by then De Ruyter had had time to reform his fleet, and twenty of the least damaged had been formed into a rearguard. These did extremely well, holding off the English through the night, and in the morning the battle was discontinued.

The English rear under Admiral Smythe and Tromp's own squadron were now locked in conflict right on the coast. Tromp had had the best of the exchanges upon first leaving his fleet, and chased Smythe through the night. On the 26th, the wind

Battaglia Nauale tra' Inglesi, et Olandesi Successa adi 13 di Giugno 1665.

More ships blow up in the great sea battle off Lowestoft. A figurehead from one of the Dutch ships is now the sign at the Red Lion Inn, Martlesham, Suffolk.

Overleaf The Four Days' Battle of Sole Bay (Southwold), 11–14 June 1666. Tactics appear utterly confusing. The 'line of battle' of Nelson's day had not yet been evolved.

ZEE-SLAG TUSSEN D'ENGELSE EN NEERLANDERS, ONDER 'T B[

L'Admirael G. M. de Ruyter.

1. den H.' Adm.' de Ruyter de Vloot passeerende doet de Engelsen ruymen.
2. Een Engels Schip vande blaeuwe Vlag van tusse de 60 en. 70 Stucken bij de Adm.' d'Ruyt gesoncken.
3. Een Engels Schip van de Witte Vlag gesoncken.
4. den L. Adm.' Tromp sich dapper op verscheyde Sche: pen gequasten hebbende, vaert na
5. 't Schip Gouda van de Schout bij nacht Sweers en verovert.
6. de Royal Prince gevoert door S.' Georg Ascue

Al.'vande witte Vlag welck Schip naderhant is verbrant en den Lord Ascue in Hollant gevanckelyck opgebracht.
7. den Luijt Adm.' Cornelis Evertse pogende
8. den Schout bij Nacht vande witte Vlag een brander aen boort te brengen
9. 't Schip van Cap.' Pieter Salomonsz verbr.'
10. de Vice Admirael de Liefde
11. Een Engels Schip vande witte Vlag door de Liefde soo doorschoten dat schuyns op de wint:

veeren van de Liefde sonck.

12. 't Schip de Nagelboom verovert door

13. de Vice Admirael Coenders.

14. Cap. Hendrick Adriaans verovert.

15. Sr William Berkley Vice Adl vande witte Vlag met 70 Stucken. 16. Cap. vander Zaen verovert

17. de Seven Wolden met 70 Stucken.

18. Een Engels Schip verbrant

19. door een Hollantsche Brander

20. Iacob Andreass. Swart verovert

21. 't Schip de Loyale George met 44 Stucken.

22. Cap. van Meuwen schiex

23. Een Engels Schip met ontrent 50 Stucken inde gront 24. 't Schip Duyvenvoorde gest. door Cap. Treslong verbrant. 25 Cap. Paeu vero. 26 tschip Essex met 58 Stucken.

27. Cap. Ruth Maximilian verovert 28. Een Engels Schip genaemt de Converteyn

29 Prins Robbert komt op den 13 Iunij met 22 Oorlogschepen tot secours van d'Engelse vloot.

Monck.

L. Admirael C. Tromp.

shifted to Smythe's favour. In the meantime, Van Tromp had heard of the defeat of the Dutch fleet and broke off the battle to run for home. This battle, the 'St James's Day Battle', resulted in the Dutch losing twenty ships and four thousand killed and three thousand wounded. The most important consequence was that it gave the English command of the seas. Another result was that the East Anglian coastal towns were becoming overrun with Dutch prisoners and English casualties. No less than sixteen hundred were imprisoned in Ipswich, together with three hundred English wounded, a quantity that the town Corporation were hard-put to deal with.

De Ruyter and the attack on Landguard

It was only a matter of two months before De Ruyter was at sea again. He was thirsting for revenge on the English and for the restoration of his country's prestige. The English fleet was at its usual anchorage at Southwold when the Dutch descended upon it. Before battle could be joined a storm blew up, separating the two opponents. This was the last action to be fought in 1666.

Peace negotiations went forward at Breda shortly after. The resulting events show quite clearly the English talent for winning the war but losing the peace. Charles II, our king, was over-confident. The Dutch had been badly knocked about at sea in a couple of actions, as we have seen, and Charles was haughty and unjust in his demands, naming terms that the Dutch could not possibly have accepted. This in itself, was unwise, as it only provoked the Dutch into a desperate resistance. But, in addition, Charles disbanded his fleet. His finances were in such a mess through his own extravagance that the government was facing penury. Charles's remedy for this was to have great numbers of the English ships taken out of commission. With the war over, as he thought, the fleet was an expensive waste of money to his luxury-loving mind. It was a mistake that has been repeated more than once in our history. As the summer of 1667 drew on, England no longer had her hundred ships-of-the-line, just two small squadrons.

The Dutch knew all this, and conceived a daring plan for striking a mortal blow at the English navy. A small fleet of about twenty sail was sent to Scottish waters to harass the privateers. Another fifty were gathered together to form the main striking force. The ruse of attacking the Scottish privateers worked, and the English had no inkling of what was really afoot. On 7 June 1667, the combined Dutch fleet was off the Gunfleet near Harwich; two days later, they entered the Thames and stormed the fort at Sheerness. On the way, they loosed off a few broadsides at East Tilbury church in Essex, damaging the tower considerably.

Three days later came the worst; while the main fleet lay in the Thames, a squadron pushed on into the Medway. On the 14th they burned the English ships that were laid up there, and carried away the flagship *Royal Charles*, pride of the English navy, as a prize. Quite justifiably, this is called the blackest day in British naval history. While part of the Dutch fleet stayed in the Thames the rest came up to cruise off the Suffolk coast.

Meanwhile, feverish preparations were going on to resist an invasion attempt. The Suffolk militia had been called out, and were camping on Walton Heights, Felixstowe, so as to be able to defend the Orwell estuary. This aroused the protests of Southwold and Aldeburgh, who claimed that they were being left defenceless. At Aldeburgh the inhabitants fled their homes until four companies of troops were sent there. What was lacking was artillerymen; there was a fine battery of twenty guns, but nobody to work them. Southwold had only four guns mounted – another five lay useless for want of carriages – and only a few rounds of ammunition. Lowestoft had petitioned for guns, but added that the people of Lowestoft had suffered so badly from the Dutch that they were quite unable to build a battery.

Landguard fort was to be the pivot of the defence, as it was thought that the Dutch would make their landing in the Orwell. Unfortunately Landguard was in poor shape. As long ago as 1664 an Order in Council had directed the strengthening of Landguard by a further thirty pieces of artillery. These had not been sent for lack of money. The Duke of York had visited the place in March 1667, and had ordered outworks to be constructed as well as the improvement of existing portions of wall with new brick facings. These improvements had not been carried out at the time of the Dutch raid. The garrison was, however, composed of regulars: marines under Captain Nathaniel Darrell. In addition, numbers of naval gunners from Ipswich were brought down to the fort to serve the guns.

The idea of an attack on Harwich had been considered by the Dutch the previous year. There was a new naval dockyard there (the crane installed in this shipyard can still be seen at Harwich), and consequently it afforded a a strategic target. But there had been some hesitation because of the presence at sea of the Royal Navy. Now, with the Navy destroyed in the Medway, there was nothing to hinder the Dutch attack. Fortunately for England, Admiral de Ruyter spent all of June prevaricating. He was unsure whether to attack Harwich, Plymouth or Portsmouth, and it was not until 30 June that the decision to attack Harwich was taken. Once this was decided, De Ruyter moved quickly. Two squadrons had been blockading the Suffolk coast for a fortnight, and on 1 July De Ruyter brought the rest of the fleet up to the rendezvous off Aldeburgh. They lay there for a day while the plan of attack was worked out. As it would be impossible to enter the Orwell in the face of opposition from Landguard, the Dutch planned to drop an assault force to storm it by land before entering the estuary.

In the event, everything went wrong. The fleet weighed anchor the next morning and were off Felixstowe by 11 a.m. As the landing had to be made out of range of the guns of Landguard, the spot chosen for the disembarkation was the stretch of beach where Felixstowe pier stands today. At 1 p.m., forty-seven of the Dutch ships drew inshore to land the men. Within the space of an hour, a thousand Dutch were ashore, with more following every minute. The plan called for no less than 3,000 to go ashore under Colonel Dolman, the English traitor who had led the assault on the Sheerness fort.

The part of the fleet which was to provide covering fire did not have the same success. The squadrons of Admirals Van Nes and Evertsen were supposed to move in close to bombard the fort from two sides; one squadron was to fire from Felixstowe Bay, the other was to move farther into the river approaches and fire at the south side. They ran into problems because all the buoys and beacons had been removed, and ships had been scuttled to block the fairways. Van Nes went aground as he advanced. By the time that he had been hauled off and put boats out to sound the passage, the wind had dropped and the tide was ebbing against him. Evertsen also had problems with the maze of shoals in Felixstowe Bay. He, in fact, never got within effective range of the fort at all.

These accidents destroyed the original scheme of providing covering fire. The landing party, who had been hanging around waiting for the ships to get into position, now began to have their own worries. The delay had given the Suffolk militia, under James, Earl of Suffolk, time to come up. Instead of attempting any tricky manoeuvres, James wisely had his men line the cliff top overlooking the beach-head and start a heavy skirmishing fire upon the Dutch. Where Wolsey Gardens and Convalescent Hill are today, the Suffolk musketeers swarmed, thoroughly disorganizing the Dutch at little cost to themselves.

With his plan falling to pieces around him, De Ruyter came ashore. There seemed little point in wasting any more time, so he ordered the assault on Landguard to go forward without the preliminary bombardment from the ships. Leaving one thousand men to return the fire of the Suffolk militia, De Ruyter led the storming party, weighed down with ladders, towards the fort. They went down what is now Langer Road and formed up at 5 p.m. on the marshes which today are all Ministry of Defence property. The assault when it came lasted for three-quarters of an hour. For all that time the Dutch attempted to get their ladders against the walls, while the garrison fired steadily back at them. The turning point came when two small English sloops lying in the river hit upon the idea of firing their cannons into the shingle. With a blizzard of stinging stones whistling about them, the Dutch withdrew to a depression in the ground. They were rallied, and tried one more assault at 7 p.m. This was a half-hearted effort that lasted only minutes and the attackers withdrew, leaving their scaling ladders behind. When they returned to the beach, the tide was out and the ships were unable to come in to take them off. It was 2 a.m. the following day before the last Dutchman left: the Suffolk militia had harried them for every single minute until then. But the Dutch did make their withdrawal, though the day's work at Felixstowe had cost them 150 casualties.

De Ruyter returned to the Thames, and fought one more action off the Essex coast before the year's campaigning was done. On 23 July, a Dutch flotilla probed up the Hope, an Essex tributary of the Thames that is now underground, and found there a squadron of small ships which were awaiting the arrival of their new commander, Sir Edward Spragge. Admiral van Nes attacked, using up thirteen of his fireships in return for six of the English vessels destroyed. The English were driven to take shelter under the guns of Tilbury fort. The next day, Sir Edward Spragge arrived. He attacked the Dutch and drove them right away from Tilbury. When he was joined by the Harwich flotilla, the Dutch retreated, although they still hovered off the coast. Before there could be any more engagements, peace was signed at Breda on 31 July, bringing matters to a conclusion.

The Third Dutch War

Less than five years later, we were at war with the Dutch again. After Breda, England, Holland and Sweden had acted in concert to prevent Louis XIV of France from swallowing up the old Spanish Netherlands. Louis bribed Charles II with the promise of territory on the Continent if England would help France against the Dutch. As a result, Charles provoked the Third Dutch War, which began on 19 March 1672. This conflict was different from the previous ones for a number of reasons. France was our ally, and this alone made the war extremely unpopular. In addition, this was not just a maritime struggle, as the French intended to overrun Holland.

The Duke of York led the combined Anglo-French fleet, which was formed in May. Though there were ninety-eight battleships in the fleet, it was seriously weakened by internal disputes. The two nationalities were mutually critical and full of suspicion about their relative fighting ability. It was this hatred of one another that was to be so weakening when the time came to meet the Dutch.

De Ruyter was leading the Dutch fleet again. During this war he was to show himself a genius, and it is largely due to him that Holland escaped disaster. In May 1672, he sailed with a fleet of seventy-five ships into the North Sea. He found the Anglo-French fleet on 19 May, anchored at the Gunfleet off Harwich. The weather was thick, and contact was soon lost. Instead of taking any aggressive action, James simply sailed into Southwold Bay and had the fleet anchor in a north–south line parallel to the coast. The French ships formed the southern part of the line, the Earl of Sandwich the northern, while James's squadron made up the centre. There they stayed until, on 26 May, they received a report that the Dutch had returned home.

The next day the wind began to blow savagely from the north-east. A council of war was being held aboard the flagship, HMS *Prince*, and the Earl of Sandwich suggested that the fleet should put to sea for fear of being pinned against the shore by the wind. Not only did the Duke of York refuse the suggestion – after all, he had heard that the Dutch were nowhere near, so who was going to attack the fleet? – but he also made the quite unpardonable accusation that it had been prompted by cowardice on the part of Sandwich. Within hours, Sandwich's foreboding came true.

At three o'clock that afternoon, a French craft on look-out duty to the north-east came scudding back into Southwold Bay under all sail. The news it brought was that the Dutch were approaching, and would be on the combined fleet within the hour. The Anglo-French had been caught entirely unprepared. Large parties of men were ashore with watering gangs, and most of the fleet's boats were engaged in routine duties around the battleships. Sandwich was more prepared than the rest, and he wasted no time. Not even bothering to spend precious minutes in weighing anchor, he simply cut his cables and clawed out of the bay on the starboard tack (i.e. towards the north). Soon the Dutch fleet was in sight to the east-north-east. It was a majestic sight as it bore down on Sandwich's squadron, being drawn up in line abreast, instead of the usual line ahead. In the first line were the fireships, covered by eighteen ships-of-the-line. Behind that came the main part of the fleet; on the left was Admiral Banckers, on the right, Admiral van Ghent, while De Ruyter himself led the centre.

Sandwich moved against the Dutch right, hoping to buy time for the combined fleet to get into some kind of order. Although he did his best, the allies were really only saved from disaster by the wind suddenly dropping. While it was light, the Duke of York stood out of Southwold Bay, taking the starboard tack, as Sandwich had done. The French, however, took the port tack, and stood out towards the south-east, so that a gap rapidly widened between the English and French ships. It is quite likely that this was a deliberate move, in accordance with secret orders from Paris that the king's fine new ships were not to be risked in battle. De Ruyter, who had experience of the value of the French as allies, took advantage of their lack of heart and despatched only a tiny portion of his fleet to engage them, leaving him with fifty-five ships against the English sixty-five.

While the wind was so light and variable, and the great ships lay dead in the water, the English got their boats out and towed the ships into some kind of order by the muscle-power of the rowers alone. Then the wind freshened again, blowing not from the north-east any more, but from the south-east. This gave the English all the sea-room they needed to the northward. Twice the wind had favoured the English; first by dying away before the Dutch could press into Southwold Bay, now by changing direction so that the English had room to manoeuvre away from the coast.

As the battle was joined, the Duke of York closed with De Ruyter in the centre. Sandwich's *Royal James* was attacked by the *Groot Hollandia* which, though only half the strength of the English ship,

The Battle of Sole Bay was a draw, largely because the French, England's allies, kept out of the action. Many buildings were commandeered to house the Dutch prisoners taken in the battle, including the Bell and Steelyard Inn, Woodbridge.

managed to disable two-thirds of the English crew. It was a splendid attack, pressed home with courage; but gradually the hundred guns of the *Royal James* began to batter down the opposition. Just as Sandwich was gaining the upper hand, Admiral van Ghent intervened. For two hours the two flagships slogged it out. Van Ghent himself was killed and victory was assured to Sandwich. Then, the *Royal James* was engaged again. This time a fireship successfully grappled her, setting her ablaze. Sandwich held her until the last, then entered a longboat to transfer to another ship. This was packed with frightened survivors and overturned. Sandwich was among the drowned; his body, recognizable only by the Star of the Order of St George on its chest, was recovered a few days later.

Sandwich's fight had demoralized the Dutch rear, which retired when news of Van Ghent's death got around. This retreat left the two English squadrons (the French were still keeping well away from the fighting) able to concentrate against De Ruyter. The fight continued until dark, and was so severe that the smoke from the cannon drifted down as far as the Essex coast. The Dutch drew off to the north in good order. Next day, they were still there, and the English closed with them for action. The

'Bloody Flagg' for the order to commence firing was already up when a sudden sea mist came down. In it, the Dutch escaped home.

The battle of Solebay was claimed by both sides as a victory. The fairest way to assess it is as a draw. The English were left in possession of the field, and took the Dutch ship *Stavaren*. The Dutch, on the other hand, had prevented the enemy from crossing the North Sea to co-operate with the French troops in the Netherlands–an achievement of incalculable value. It was, as De Ruyter said, a most obstinate fight.

8

THE EIGHTEENTH CENTURY

The county regiments

AFTER the Dutch Wars, our attention must shift from East Anglian places to East Anglian units. The regular regiments with which we are concerned are the 9th, 12th, 30th, 44th and 56th Foot; respectively the Royal Norfolks, the Suffolks, the Cambridge-shires and the East and West Essex Regiments. Of course, each unit went through a number of stages before emerging as a county regiment, and so the original units may have had little to do with East Anglia. Nevertheless, as the ancestors of our local regulars, they deserve some attention.

Both the Norfolks and the Suffolks were raised at the same time, in 1685. In those days each regiment was known only by its Colonel's name. The Norfolks, for instance, were respectively Cornwall's, Purcell's, Cunningham's and Steuart's. The Suffolks were actually raised from Suffolk men by the Duke of Norfolk. Later, they became Litchfield's, Brewer's and Livesay's. Both regiments fought together in Ireland during King William's war, and both were present at the Battle of the Boyne.

War of the Spanish Succession

A few years later the Norfolks were in Spain during the War of the Spanish Succession, as was a new regiment, Colonel Saunderson's Regiment of Marines, who were to become the Cambridgeshire Regiment. It was at the battle of Almanza in 1707 that the Norfolks first distinguished themselves. They were so prominent in the thick of the fighting against the Spanish and French that they were barely one hundred strong when they returned to England. Almanza is supposed to be where the Norfolks first adopted the figure of Britannia as the regimental badge. The exact reason for this remains unknown. What is certain is that the regiment was

given *official* permission to use this badge in 1799, and the 'ancient' use of the badge is alluded to, so Almanza may well be where this tradition originated. Bearing this in mind, it is obvious why the regimental march is 'Rule Britannia'. After Almanza it was to be fifty-four years before the regiment saw active service again.

War of the Austrian Succession

In 1713, both regiments took a step towards their eventual titles of Norfolks and Suffolks by being accepted 'into the line' as the 9th and 12th Regiments of foot. It was not to be long before the 12th were imitating the steadiness in battle that the 9th had shown. In 1742, the 12th left for Europe to take part in the War of the Austrian Succession. On 27 June of the next year, with the army engaged in a strategic withdrawal in the face of a superior enemy, the French stood in the path of the English at Dettingen on the River Maine. The battle which followed is the last occasion on which an English monarch led his troops in battle. In the centre of the English line were the 12th, and George II dismounted and placed himself at their head. Though they had been on a starvation diet because of a failure of supplies, there was no stopping the English infantry that day, and the French fled in confusion. As a result of the battle, the 12th wore laurel leaves (later roses) both on the Sovereign's birthday and in the presence of the Sovereign. In addition, in the middle of the last century, they were allowed to wear a crown on their shakoes as well as the normal regimental number.

The '45 Rebellion

The next duty of the 12th was to be in Scotland, where the landing of Bonnie Prince Charlie had

Admiral Rooke captures Gibraltar, 23 July 1704. During the great siege of 1779–83 the 12th and 56th from East Anglia fought doggedly to retain the Rock in British hands.

England in an uproar. In fact, the Jacobites had already badly mauled one East Anglian Regiment. This was the 44th, later the East Essex Regiment, which had been raised in 1741 by Colonel Long, and which was quartered around Colchester. In 1744, the regiment was sent north with General Cope when the landing of the Prince first became known. At Prestonpans, Cope was attacked in the mist by the wild Highlanders who had closed up under cover of night. Though the infantry managed to fire two good volleys, the day was lost for them once the Scots got close enough to use their claymores. It took only ten minutes for the English to be completely routed.

Fighting the French in America

Some ten years later the 44th was to be badly cut up again. In January 1755, the regiment was sent to America to help counteract the growing French menace. The commander of the force was General Edward Braddock, a narrow-minded martinet who was quite unsuited to wilderness warfare. The 44th was landed at Alexandria in Virginia with the object of attacking Fort Duquesne (modern Pittsburgh), to sever the line of French fortresses which ran from Canada to the Ohio. The whole force, about 2,200 men, set out through the forest, and was ambushed on 8 July by a force of Indians in the pay of the French. A withering fire was opened on them by an invisible enemy and soon the English were in desperate trouble. Braddock refused to let his men take cover behind the trees, and had them lined up in correct European fashion where they made a perfect target for the concealed enemy marksmen. As soon as Braddock himself was shot, the whole force broke from the field.

The Seven Years War

Four years later, during the Seven Years War, the 12th were engaged in the battle for which they are chiefly remembered. On 1 August, at Minden in Germany, a force of English and Hanoverians met the French. There were six English infantry regiments there, and they were ordered to take the village of Hahlen. They misunderstood the order and, in two lines with the 12th in the front line, they advanced straight at the heart of the French army. They passed steadily through a scorching artillery crossfire of sixty-six guns to where ten thousand French cavalry waited for them. The French horsemen were the pride of the army. In their beautiful uniforms, they came thundering down on the English regiments, intending to cut them to pieces. At thirty paces, the infantry gave them a volley that brought the whole mass to a halt. Six times more the French charged, and each time the terrible musketry of the steady troops brought them up short. Finally, the whole seventy-five French squadrons retreated in a boiling, disordered mob. Next, two brigades of French infantry tried to intervene, only to meet the same fate as the cavalry. The English were then attacked by a large force of Saxons, and these too were defeated. The French Marshal Contades said that he had never seen such a thing before – 'A single line of infantry break through three lines of cavalry and throw them into confusion.' That day cost the regiment 302 men killed and wounded out of a strength of 480. Minden Day is still celebrated in the British Army. The six regiments, as they advanced, had plucked roses to wear in their hats. This tradition has survived, and the regiments involved in the battle wear roses every 1 August.

American War of Independence

The last of the East Anglian Regiments was raised in 1756. This was Manners' Regiment, the 56th. They were with the 9th in 1762, also during the Seven Years War, when an attack was mounted on Cuba. Havana was taken without much trouble, but the army suffered terrible casualties through sickness. During the next war, the American War of Independence, which also included fighting in Europe, the 56th were to serve with another local unit – the 12th. Both were present at the Great Siege of Gibraltar, which lasted from 1779–83. Almost all this time they were under attack from superior Spanish forces. The ultimate attack, made by specially-constructed floating batteries, was put to flight by the use of red-hot shot. In 1784, the king approved the honour 'Gibraltar' to be worn on the colours. In addition, the 12th adopted the Castle of Gibraltar as the design for the regimental badge.

All the other East Anglian units fought in North America. The 44th were with General Howe in 1776, and took part in the fighting for New York and Long Island. During the winter, they formed part of a force sent out to raid Washington's supply base at Danbury. On their return march they were terribly harassed by American backwoodsmen, and suffered severely. They were part of Howe's army which attacked Philadelphia that autumn. Finding his way barred at Brandywine Creek, Howe sent General Cornwallis with the 44th to turn the American flank, and won a very neat victory. The 30th went to America in 1781 as part of General Clinton's reinforcements, and took part in the fighting in Carolina and Georgia.

The Norfolks were to have the most disastrous role during this war. They operated out of Canada, and were present at the Battle of Three Rivers in 1776. Next year they were with General Burgoyne, and surrendered with him at Saratoga. They spent the rest of the war as prisoners. They were repatriated in 1781, and brought their colours back with them. At Saratoga, Lieutenant-Colonel Hill, their commanding officer, had hidden the colours in his baggage. On returning to England he presented them to the king.

The Napoleonic Wars

The next year, 1782, saw an important administrative step in the history of the British Army. In August, the king decreed that each regiment known only by its number should henceforth bear the name of a county, with which it would establish close relations. As the king put it: 'so as to create a mutual attachment between the county and the regiment which may at all times be useful towards recruiting the regiment.' Thus, as the Napoleonic Wars opened, the 9th was the East Norfolk Regiment, the 12th was the East Suffolk, the 30th was the Cambridgeshire Regiment, the 44th was the East Essex, and the 56th was the West Essex.

The Napoleonic and French Revolutionary Wars lasted for twenty-three years almost continuously. Such was the scale of the fighting that only certain incidents which involved East Anglian units can be mentioned here. The Norfolks were in the West

The Battle of
Dettingen, 1743. This
was the last occasion
on which a British
monarch personally
led his troops in
battle. The 12th Foot
(Suffolks) played a
notable part in the
victory.

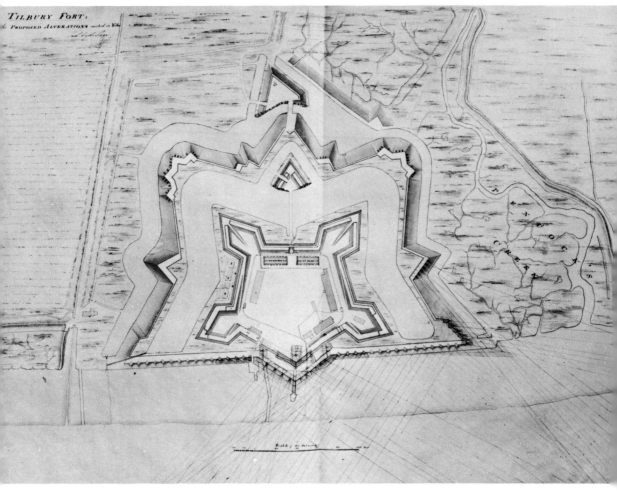

Plan for the improvement of Tilbury Fort, approved 12 June 1778. Originally built by Henry VIII, the ruins can be seen today. The church nearby houses a memorial to the garrison.

Opposite In 1782 the 56th Foot became the West Essex Regiment. The engraving shows an officer of 1798. Regiments of the British Army were distinguished by the colour of cuffs, lapels and turnbacks, and by the design of the lace.

Indies, the Suffolks were bogged down in the Flanders campaign, and the Cambridgeshires were facing young Captain Bonaparte at the Siege of Toulon in 1793–4, which gives some idea of the range of the hostilities.

In 1800, the government became worried by the presence of a French army in Egypt, which threatened our communications with India. In March 1801, a British expeditionary force, which included the East Essex and Cambridgeshires, was landed at Aboukir Bay, scene of the naval Battle of the Nile three years before. On 21 March, a battle was fought in which the French were utterly defeated. In recognition of their services the regiments

involved were allowed to use the sphinx superscribed 'Egypt' as part of the regimental badge.

These years were also the years when invasion seemed likely. In August 1793 a force of Yeomanry was raised at Bury St Edmunds. This was known as the Suffolk Light Dragoons, designed to protect the county in the event of invasion. Eventually, there were no less than forty-two militia companies scattered over Suffolk. At the same time, the East Essex Militia was put on permanent service, acting as a garrison for the important military sites in Essex, such as the large camp raised just outside Chelmsford. The Militia were splendid in uniform, wearing red coats faced with green. A new force was

56TH REGIMENT OF FOOT, 1798.

raised in 1798, the 'Sea Fencibles', which was designed as a kind of floating militia – the object of the force being to provide a reserve of seamen to act as crews for a 'last ditch' effort to stop the French invasion barges. For a time their commander was Admiral Nelson, but relations between him and them were never amicable. The Fencibles were in fact a commander's nightmare: amateurish, incompetent and riddled with shirkers seeking the easiest way to serve England.

Yarmouth was a naval base of some importance during these years. It was the headquarters for the North Sea squadron, whose main duty consisted in watching the Dutch coast, which was in the hands of the French. It was from Yarmouth that Admiral Duncan sailed to win the battle of Camperdown in 1798, and it was to Yarmouth that he returned with the Dutch prizes. Yarmouth was also the base from

which the Copenhagen expedition of 1801 was launched. This fleet, under Admiral Sir Hyde Parker, with Nelson as a subordinate, met tragedy before it left East Anglian waters.

Yarmouth was a tricky roadstead for the big ships of the line. Situated just north of the town, the roadstead was protected to seaward by large sandbanks and shoals which were constantly shifting. The first part of the fleet sailed via St Nicholas' Channel, and used local pilots. The second squadron came up from the Downs and called in to Yarmouth to pick up its orders. Parker had not sent the orders down to them as he should, with the result that the squadron had to anchor in the roads at Yarmouth quite unnecessarily. Picking up a pilot, the ships attempted to run out not by the south-east channel but through the dangerous Cockle Gateway. In a heavy sea, HMS *Invincible*, with Rear Admiral

Burial of Sir John Moore at Corunna, 1809, by the Norfolk Regiment. Compelled to retreat through the mountains before the vastly superior numbers of the French, Sir John turned and delivered a sharp check to Marshal Soult to cover the British embarkation. Engraving by Edmund Evans.

Opposite The 9th (East Norfolk) Regiment in the Peninsular War. The Colour Sergeant (left) protects with his pike the Ensign bearing the Regimental Colours.

Totty aboard, hit Hammond's Knoll sandbank. Dismasted, she wallowed there while the local fishing smacks attempted to give assistance. They rescued some, but with night falling and the sea rising, were forced to lay off. Next day the *Invincible* sank, taking four hundred men down with her.

A number of the defences raised against invasion can still be seen on the Suffolk coast. A British expedition to the Mediterranean, which included the Cambridgeshire Regiment, had suffered at Corsica in trying to take a defensive tower. The strength of this so impressed the British that the design was copied when a number of strongpoints were erected on the exposed east coast. Called Martello Towers, the ones erected in Suffolk were numbered L–Z, with three more, AA, BB, and CC. In form they are round towers about fifty feet high, with immensely thick walls. Originally they mounted either three twenty-four pounder cannon, or one cannon and two howitzers. There were three at Aldeburgh, and some fine examples survive around the mouth of the Deben at Shingle Street. In the Orwell there was one at Harwich and another at the modern naval training school HMS *Ganges*. The modern water tower is built on top of it. One of the most interesting of the towers is Dooley Fort, on the Orwell at Felixstowe. Here a battery was raised around the tower, and it is this battery that remains there today.

For most people, the Napoleonic Wars bring to mind the campaigns in the Peninsula. Three East Anglian Regiments fought in that war: the Norfolks, the East Essex and the Cambridgeshires. The Norfolks first distinguished themselves at Rolica, where an impressive charge scattered Delaborde's Division and saved the Worcestershire Regiment from virtual annihilation. After the dreadful retreat to Corunna in the winter of 1808–9, it was the Norfolks who buried the body of the commanding General, Sir John Moore, outside the town.

The exploits of the army under Wellington are so well known as to need no elaboration here. The three East Anglian units served with the 5th Division under General Leith. At the Battle of Salamanca, in 1812, the Essex Regiment captured the Eagle of the French 62nd Regiment. In honour of this exploit, the Essex Regiment still wears an Eagle collar badge.

After the end of the Peninsular War the Norfolks were sent to Canada, thus missing the Battle of Waterloo, at which both the 30th and 44th were present. As Waterloo is probably the best-known battle in English military history, a few words about the rôle of the two East Anglian Regiments will not be out of place. The 44th were in action first that day. As part of Pack's Brigade of Sir Thomas Picton's Division, they were stationed along the road behind the farm of La Haye Sainte. They were ordered to lie down to obtain some protection from the French artillery fire. When the French infantry of General D'Erlon did attack, they pushed through the British first line almost to the road where Picton's Division was. Suddenly the whole Division rose to its feet and poured a terrible volley into the French column, sending it reeling in confusion.

The 30th formed part of Colin Halkett's Brigade of Alten's Division. They were to be involved in the last attack of the last battle of the Napoleonic Wars. At 7 p.m. Napoleon made his last gamble, and committed the bearskinned veterans of the Imperial Guard to the attack. They advanced straight at the part of the line held by Halkett's Brigade. The 30th were still formed up in a square with the 73rd when the Guard hit them. Unable to withstand the pressure, they were driven back until the Foot Guards intervened to send the French crashing.

This was the last battle fought by British troops in Europe for a century. Henceforth, the East Anglian units would be defending the frontiers of the British Empire.

9

EMPIRE WARS AND WORLD WARS

AFTER the battles of the eighteenth century, culminating in Waterloo, the history of the nineteenth century seems to lack any interesting actions. Most of the history of the East Anglian regiments during this period is simply a long list of garrison duties in the outposts of Empire, punctuated by occasional punitive expeditions or frontier wars. There are, however, exceptions to this general picture, and the operations in Afghanistan in 1839–42 furnish a good example of both imperial policy and a frontier war.

The Afghan Wars

In the Regimental chapel of the Essex Regiment at Little Warley, a scrap of flag flies in a glass case on the chancel wall. It bears the battle honour 'Badajos', but is intimately linked with the events of 1841. The British government had always feared Russian expansion into India. As a means of checkmating any such designs, the government decided to set up a buffer against Russia in the shape of the Afghans and other tribes of the North-West Frontier. The drawback to this was the fact that the Afghan ruler, Dost Mahomed, hated the British. This matter was quickly taken care of – Dost Mahomed was replaced by Shah Shuja, a friendly prince who entered Afghanistan with the British invasion force in 1839. For the next two years Kabul, the capital, had a British garrison to keep the prince on his throne. Among the garrison was a battalion, seven hundred strong, of the 44th East Essex Regiment.

Two years later, the country rose in revolt, prompted by Dost Mahomed's son, Akber Khan. After the murder of two British diplomats, General Elphinstone decided to withdraw from Afghanistan, and was promised a safe passage. In December the column, encumbered with wives, families, and other refugees, set out through the snow-bound mountain passes. On the way the Afghans fell on

them, sniping from the hillsides and looting the dead. Of the sixteen thousand people there only a handful escaped. The Essex Regiment marched doggedly as the rearguard. Finally, near Gundamuk, the remnants made their last stand. There was only one survivor, the Ensign, Thomas Souter. He had wrapped the colours around his body like a sash. Wounded, he lay expecting death. Miraculously, an Afghan warrior took a fancy to Souter's telescope and spared him. He was later rescued, and the remaining scrap of the colours came home to the Regimental chapel.

When the news of the massacre got out, General Pollock led a punitive expedition which included the Norfolk Regiment. The problem that faced Pollock was that the Afghans were holding the Khyber Pass in strength, and this was a position that would be difficult or even impossible to penetrate. In the event, the Khyber Pass was stormed by the Norfolks. The Afghans sniped at them from the precipices and hurled huge rocks down, but it was the bayonets of the 9th that finally sent the tribesmen running. Once through the pass, the Norfolks passed the terrible sight of the hundreds of mouldering skeletons of the annihilated Elphinstone column.

The loss of the *Birkenhead*

One of the first flags borne by the Suffolks carried the inscription 'Stabilis', which means 'Steady'. This motto notably sums up the conduct of a contingent of the regiment at the beginning of 1852, when the *Birkenhead*, a paddle-wheeled transport, set sail for South Africa. Aboard her were almost four hundred soldiers, including fifty-five men of

The 9th Foot (who became the Norfolks) mount a bayonet charge at the Battle of Ferozham, 22 December 1845.

the Suffolk Regiment en route to join the regiment in fighting the Kaffir War. Off the coast of Africa the *Birkenhead* smashed into a reef, broke almost in two, and slowly began to slide below the waves. Many of the lifeboats had been wrecked in the collision, and only three remained seaworthy. The soldiers stood absolutely steady as the women and children filled the boats and pushed off. Many of the men knew that they faced certain death – most could not swim, and the boats were the only chance of leaving the *Birkenhead* alive. Knowing that the boats would be swamped if any more tried to get in, the troops stood steadily on the heeling deck until the *Birkenhead* sank. A few, clinging to wreckage, did survive: most fell victim to sharks or their own exhaustion.

Although not strictly a military episode at all, the loss of the *Birkenhead* must rank high in the honours of the Suffolk Regiment. There is a memorial tablet commemorating the incident. It can still be seen on the wall of St Mary's Church, Bury St Edmunds.

Cardwell Army reforms

In 1881 the East Anglian Regiments underwent their last re-organization. In that year, a series of changes known as the Cardwell Reforms came into effect. The basic reform was that every English infantry regiment was to have two battalions, bear the name of a county, and have that county area as its recruiting base. This meant that many regiments were amalgamated with others to provide the necessary two battalions. In effect there was no change to the 9th Norfolks and 12th Suffolks, as the older English Regiments all had two battalions anyway. (Actually, the names of these two regiments were changed from the official East Norfolks and East Suffolks to the plain Norfolks and Suffolks.) To the two Essex Regiments, East and West, it meant amalgamation. The 44th (East Essex) became the 1st Battalion the Essex Regiment; the 56th (West Essex) became the 2nd Battalion. The new regiment adopted as its badge a design that incorporated two honours of its constituent battalions before amalgamation. The Castle and Keys of

Typical of the Victorian infantry, called upon to fight all over the world to defend the frontiers of the Empire, are these men of the Essex Regiment (44th and 56th Foot) pictured in the *Army and Navy Gazette* of 1894. The scarlet coat they wear was abandoned less than ten years later during the Boer War and replaced by khaki to make 'Tommy Atkins' a less conspicuous target.

World War I. The 2nd Battalion Norfolks man an outpost on the Jebel Hamrin.

Gibraltar (commemorating the role of the 56th during the Great Siege) appear, surrounded by a wreath of oak leaves. At the top of the oak leaves is the sphinx badge, awarded to the 44th for its service in the Egyptian campaign of 1801.

The fate of the Cambridgeshire regiment is rather more sad. It was linked with the East Lancashire Regiment, and ceased to be an East Anglian Regiment. In fact, Cambridgeshire was left without a regular regiment. This was offset to some extent in 1908, when the Territorial Army was formed. The Cambridgeshire Rifle Volunteers, formed in 1860 and made the 3rd (Volunteer) Battalion of the Suffolk Regiment in 1887, was given the title 'The Cambridgeshire Regiment'. It was associated with the Suffolks for training purposes, and shared the

Suffolks' Regimental march, 'Speed the Plough'.

The other basic idea behind the Cardwell System was that, of the two battalions of a regiment, one would be on active service abroad, while the other would be at home, recruiting, training, and possibly sending reinforcements out to its sister battalion abroad.

The First World War

This was the situation when the First World War broke out in 1914. Very quickly, as the magnitude of the conflict demanded more and more men, the old two-battalion regiments were superseded by huge multi-battalion units: the Suffolks, for in-

stance, fielded twenty-seven battalions and the Norfolks twenty. In this way we find elements of each regiment present in almost every theatre of the war – the Western Front, Gallipoli, Mesopotamia, Palestine, and so on. For this reason, a list of the various actions in which East Anglian units participated is too lengthy to enumerate here. One interesting fact that must be mentioned, however, is that at the Battle of Le Cateau, in 1914, the Suffolks were opposed to a German Regiment which had evolved from Hardenburg's Hanoverian Regiment. What was particularly sad about this encounter was that Hardenburg's Regiment had advanced in support of the Suffolks at Minden, and wore the Minden Rose. The same regiment had also formed part of the garrison of Gibraltar during the Great Siege.

At home there was fear of a deadly new weapon – the airship. East Anglia had already been bombarded from the sea. In November 1914, Yarmouth was bombarded, and this was followed some eighteen months later by the shelling of Lowestoft. On that occasion sixty 11-inch shells were fired at the town. Southwold, which was attacked in January 1917, fared better. Of seventy shells fired, only four hit the town. The airships were a new weapon. They ranged over East Anglia, attempting to bomb the munitions factories in our area. The first raid was made in January 1915, and soon it was realized that the Zeppelins always followed the same route, crossing the coast between Happisburgh and Tremingham. Consequently the defence, which included searchlights and machine-guns, was centred on Bacton. The defences never had a great deal of success and only two airships were brought down over East Anglia during the war. One came down at Little Wigburgh in Essex, in September 1916. The other was shot down by a fighter from Orford-ness in June 1917, at Theberton, near Leiston. The raids did little harm. The greatest amount of damage occurred in September 1916, when fourteen Zeppelins crossed the coast to drop a total of sixteen tons of bombs.

There were also one or two seaplane attacks on the naval air base at Great Yarmouth. A more serious attack was mounted against the seaplane base at Felixstowe in 1917 by German Gotha bombers. Seventeen people were killed in this attack.

When peace was declared in 1918, the destroyers and submarines of the German fleet were brought into Harwich to surrender. One needs only to look at the War Memorials in East Anglian towns to see

Zeppelins over East Anglia. Compared with the bomb load of later aircraft airships carried a small dose of destruction. But they could inflict real damage. This picture shows their effect at Yarmouth in 1915.

Opposite Airships, the terrifying new weapon, brought home to the people of East Anglia the stark reality of war. Men of the Norfolk Regiment (note the Britannia hat badge) have recovered this bomb fragment from ruins of a struck building.

Overleaf The 7th Suffolk Regiment in World War I. Suffolks in the ruins of Tilloy Church in France, 18 October 1917.

Surrender of the German High Seas Fleet at the Armistice of 1918. The submarines and destroyers were brought to Harwich and here the crew of a German submarine are seen transferring to a motor launch.

the sacrifice of local men. More than five thousand were killed in the Norfolk Regiment alone – and a third of that number died in the Battle of the Somme. Once more the regiments were reduced to two battalions, the extra wartime battalions being disbanded and laying up their colours in the Regimental chapels.

There is little to interest us between the two World Wars, except to note that in 1935 the Norfolk Regiment was granted the distinction 'Royal', and was henceforth to be known as the Royal Norfolk Regiment. This was granted in the year which marked George V's twenty-fifth year on the throne. It was also 250 years since Cornwall's Regiment of Foot had been first raised.

The Second World War

With the outbreak of the Second World War, in 1939, the East Anglian Regiments were at once brought up to wartime strength again, though they never grew as large as they had been in the First World War. The old Yeomanry units, absorbed into the Territorial Army, were now artillery units. The Norfolks and Suffolk Yeomanry, amalgamated as an artillery brigade between the wars, were split again. The Norfolks became the 65th Anti-Tank Regiment, the Suffolks the 409th Anti-Aircraft Battery. Another battalion of the Suffolk Regiment proper, the 7th, was equipped with tanks and fought in North Africa as the 142nd Regiment of the Royal Armoured Corps.

As in the Great War, East Anglian battalions were in action in every field of operations. The 2nd Norfolks were almost wiped out at Dunkirk, not in action but in cold blood. About ninety men were captured by a German Waffen-SS unit at Le Paradis, and were machine-gunned quite murderously. Two men survived the massacre, and the German officer responsible was hanged after the war on their evidence.

One of the most disastrous battles of the war was the fall of Singapore. There were three Norfolk and two Suffolk battalions there, as well as both battalions of the Territorial Cambridgeshire Regiment. The Cambridge men were committed to fighting on the Malayan mainland, and were surrounded at Batu Pahat. They broke out, and retreated to Singapore Island, where they were in line next to the Suffolks. On 11 February 1942, the Japanese launched a heavy attack on the Suffolks on the Adam-Ferrer Road, and on the 14th the Suffolks were pushed back, leaving the flank of the Cambridgeshires exposed. The flank was held, but even this desperate defence did no good, and Singapore surrendered next day. The drums of the Cambridge Regiment, lost in the fighting, were miraculously found in a Malayan jungle thicket after the war. They were returned to the Regiment but have never been played since. Instead they are paraded with the Regiment in silence, as a tribute to the men who died in the Far East.

During the Second World War, invasion became a real fear again. Far more than in the Great War, East Anglia was the scene of sea and air actions. The coast of East Anglia was known as 'E-Boat Alley' because the fast German boats were engaged in attacks against the East Coast convoys for most of the war. East Anglia, in turn, became the home of a number of Motor Torpedo Boat squadrons. Boats were based, among other places, at Felixstowe, Ipswich, Yarmouth and Lowestoft. Another coastal force with intimate connections with East Anglia also had its headquarters at Lowestoft. This is the Royal Naval Patrol Service, which consisted of armed trawlers and whalers crewed by fishermen. The headquarters of this force were the old Municipal Gardens at Lowestoft, known locally as the 'Sparrow's Nest'. When taken over by the navy, the Gardens became HMS *Pembroke*. Another link between the force and East Anglia is that one of the vessels, the *Staffa*, was adopted by the town of Leiston, where her guns had been made. After the war *Staffa*'s flag was presented to the town council.

There were a number of minor actions fought off our coast. One early, tragic incident occurred in November 1939. A force of German E-boats approached Harwich (which was known as HMS *Badger* to the Admiralty) and dropped mines. One of the destroyers stationed at Harwich, HMS *Gypsy*, went out to investigate. She hit a mine at the mouth of the Orwell and sank instantly with almost all hands. Many of the dead are buried in Shotley churchyard.

In March 1943, a force of E-boats was engaged off Smith's Knoll, outside Yarmouth. One blew up, and another was rammed by one of the British boats. That autumn, a force of thirty German boats ventured out of Ijmuiden to attack a convoy, but were put to flight off Cromer with heavy loss by five British MTBs.

On the same day that the Suffolks and Cambridgeshires were fighting so desperately at Singapore, 11 February 1942, six Hunt class destroyers were putting out from Harwich. The German capital ships *Scharnhorst*, *Gneisenau* and *Prinz Eugen* were attempting to run the Channel from Brest to their home port of Kiel. Thanks to incompetence on the British side, they got right through the Straits of Dover. An attack mounted from the fighter base at Coltishall in Norfolk by torpedo bombers of 42 Squadron, flown there specially for this operation, failed. The six Harwich destroyers attacked the Germans off the Dutch coast that afternoon. They scored no hits with their torpedoes, and the heavy guns of the battleship *Gneisenau* hit the little HMS *Worcester* no less than seven shattering blows. The *Worcester* had over half of her crew of 130 killed or wounded. It was only through the almost superhuman efforts of Captain and crew that she got back to Harwich at all. As she tied up at Parkstone Quay, the ratings from Shotley barracks turned out to cheer her to the echo. Despite

World War II – Monte
Cassino. Infantry of the
Essex Regiment dug in
on the slopes beneath
the famous monastery
which was ruined in the
battle.

Burma 1945. Like their fathers in World War I,
men of East Anglia fought all over the globe in
World War II. These men of the Norfolk Regiment
are disembarking from a DUKW in the crossing
of the Irrawaddy.

Opposite World War II. Drums of the 1st
Battalion, Suffolk Regiment at Haecht, 18
February 1945.

Worcester's effort, and that of the other destroyers, the German ships got home safely.

It is in the development of air that the two World Wars are so different. There were a number of important airfields in East Anglia, and even today there are still great acres of concrete in pleasant rural surroundings that mark the sites of now-deserted bases. The headquarters of Number 3 Group, Bomber Command, were at Mildenhall, now a US Air Force base. The first bombing attack of the war was launched from Wattisham, near Ipswich, which had only been opened in April 1939. The target for the Blenheims of 107 and 110 Squadrons was the German naval base at Kiel, which harboured the pocket battleship *Scheer* and the heavy cruiser *Prinz Eugen*. Later, as the tide of war turned in our favour, East Anglia saw the Lancaster bombers taking off from fields like Stradishall and Honington to bomb Germany itself. The bombers were aided by a radar homing

device called 'Oboe', which was located at Cromer. In fact, radar had been developed in East Anglia. Much of the early work was done at Orfordness, and then at Bawdsey Manor at the mouth of the Deben. Bawdsey is still in use today, and the huge modern radar scanners dominate the landscape. During the war radar posts were also built at Darsham, Stoke Holy Cross (near Norwich) and West Beckham.

Besides the bomber bases, there were a number of fighter stations. Martlesham, near Woodbridge was one of the largest. Although the Battle of Britain was fought mostly to the south of East Anglia, over Kent, Martlesham was attacked on 15 August 1940 by over one hundred German planes. Further south, at Hornchurch in Essex, was the headquarters of Number 11 Group, Fighter Command, which had responsibility for the aerial defence of London. One of the squadrons stationed there was Number 54. Once, Hornchurch

was bombed as the squadron was taking off. During the war, it was the policy to use Rochford (which is now Southend airport) as a satellite base for Hornchurch. In consequence of 54 Squadron's service there, the town of Southend adopted the squadron in 1971.

During the latter part of the war, the American airforce was stationed in East Anglia in considerable strength. One American casualty was Joseph Kennedy, eldest brother of the late President Kennedy. He was killed when his plane exploded over Saxmundham.

The last act of the war as far as East Anglia was concerned, occurred on 13 May 1945, when two German E-boats put in to HMS *Beehive* (the MTB installations at Felixstowe). From one, Admiral Karl Bruening emerged. His task was a very simple one – he had simply to arrange the procedure for the surrender of the E-boat fleet. For East Anglia, the war was over.

10

TODAY

THE disbandings, closures and rundowns of East Anglian units and bases since the war have been sad and widespread. The Defence White Paper of 1957 spelt out the end of the East Anglian Regiments as separate entities. Since the war, they had all been engaged in 'peacekeeping' roles in the world's trouble spots, including Malaya and Cyprus. The Essex Regiment laid up its colours in the church at Little Warley in 1958, to become part of the Bedfordshire and Hertfordshire Regiment, the battalion wearing an eagle collar badge to commemorate the capture of the French standard at Salamanca. A number of the colours of the Essex Militia units of the Napoleonic Wars are also to be found in Chelmsford Cathedral.

In 1959, the Suffolks and Norfolks were amalgamated as the 1st East Anglian Regiment. The colours of the old Regiments are laid up at St Mary's, Bury, and at the Regimental chapel in Norwich Cathedral.

During the sixties there were further amalgamations. The 1st East Anglian Regiment became the 1st Battalion, Royal Anglian Regiment. The 2nd Battalion of this new large regiment was provided by the old Northamptonshire and Lincolnshire Regiments, while the Essex Regiment, together with its amalgamates, the Bedfordshires and Hertfordshires, provided the 3rd Battalion. In this form the Regiment has served in Northern Ireland.

The old Territorial units eventually emerged as artillery. The Essex unit is the 304th Field Regiment, Royal Artillery (TA), while the Suffolks provide the 308th Anti-Tank Regiment, Royal Artillery (TA). The Norfolk contingent is the 389th Light Anti-Aircraft Regiment, Royal Artillery (TA). Such is the state of flux in which the forces find themselves today, that even these units are liable to disappear.

All the Regiments, by the way, have their own museums. That of the Essex Regiment is at Eagle Way, Warley, Brentwood. The Norfolks' is at the Britannia Barracks, Norwich. The Cambridgeshire Regiment has a collection in the Drill Hall, Newmarket, but also shares the Suffolks' Museum. That is located at Gibraltar Barracks, Bury.

One of the saddest naval losses to the region will be the closing of the training school HMS *Ganges* at Shotley in two years' time. *Ganges* was an old wooden ship of eighty-four guns, anchored off Shotley at the end of the last century. Eventually the establishment was moved ashore, and the mizzen mast of the old wooden ship was erected on the parade ground, and forms a landmark over the Orwell estuary today.

Many of the aerodromes have either been closed or sold and put to other uses. Some have simply been abandoned and have never been reclaimed as farming land. Occasionally one passes the vast deserted runways, now overgrown with grass. Others, such as Martlesham Heath, have been put to different uses. Martlesham is now an industrial estate and the old hangars have been converted into warehouses while the officers' quarters have become offices. Another old fighter base that is enjoying a new lease of life is Rochford which, as Southend Airport, sees thousands of holidaymakers take off from its runways.

Some bases are still operational. West Raynham is the home of 100 Squadron, which was originally formed at Wittering (Norfolk) in 1917, and today flies Canberra bombers. At Wattisham there are two squadrons, Numbers 29 and 111, which fly Lightning fighters to defend the East Coast. Mostly these days they are called out to intercept the Russian TU95s (code-named 'Bears') which fly towards our coast to gather intelligence about the new radar installations at Orfordness and other military matters.

Still other bases have been turned over to the United States Air Force. Two that spring immediately to mind are Mildenhall and Woodbridge. So today the visitor to the graveyard of the Anglo-Saxon kings of East Anglia at Sutton Hoo will find the silence shattered periodically by the roar of a plane taking off, and will see one of the huge American Phantom fighter-bombers streaking into the sky from behind the Suffolk trees. Sometimes one is tempted to wonder what the royal occupants of the graveyard would say if they could speak: it seems a far cry from their days to these, when their sleep is shattered by the planes of a nation which was not even created until a thousand years after the East Anglian kingdom fell. At other times, when snow lies thick over the Deben country, and flying is impossible, it seems that time has not moved at all from the days of the Wuffinga kings.

Go to that lonely bluff overlooking the river, and see for yourself.

Further Reading

Arbman, H., *The Vikings*, London 1961.

Ashley, M., *The Greatness of Oliver Cromwell*, London 1957.

Baker, C., *The Fighting Kings of Wessex*, London 1931.

Bartlett, C., *The Long Retreat: British Defence Policy 1945–70*, London 1972.

Bond, B., *Victorian Military Campaigns*, London 1967.

Brooks, F., *The English Naval Forces 1199–1272*, London, no date.

Carew, T., *The Royal Norfolk Regiment*, London 1967.

Chadwick, H., *The Origins of the English Nation*, Cambridge 1907.

Collier, R., *Eagle Day*, London 1966.

Cottrell, L., *The Roman Forts of the Saxon Shore*, HMSO 1954.

Cruikshank, C., *Elizabeth's Army*, Oxford 1966.

Everitt, A., *Suffolk in the Great Rebellion*, Ipswich 1960.

Falls, C., *The First World War*, London 1960.

Feilung, I., *British Foreign Policy 1660–1672*, London 1930.

Firth, C., *Cromwell's Army*, London 1962.

Fleming, P., *Invasion 1940*, London 1957.

Fox, C., *Archaeology of the Cambridge Region*, Cambridge 1946.

Freeman, E., *History of the Norman Conquest of England*, Oxford 1867–79.

Fortescue, J., *History of the British Army*, London 1910–30.

Frere, S., *Britannia*, London 1967.

Graves, C., *Britain's Home Guard*, London 1943.

Hodgkin, R., *A History of the Anglo-Saxons*, Oxford 1953.

Holmes, T., *Ancient Britain and the Invasions of Julius Caesar*, Oxford 1917.

Lindsay, A., *A Portrait of Britain Before 1066*, Oxford 1963.

Liversedge, J., *Britain in the Roman Empire*, London 1968.

Mattingley, G., *The Defeat of the Spanish Armada*, London 1959.

Mitchell, J., *Great Britain: Geographical Essays*, Cambridge 1962.

Moir, R., *The Antiquity of Man in East Anglia*, Cambridge 1926.

Norgate, K., *John Lackland*, London 1902.

Orr, M., *Dettingen*, London 1972.

Roots, I., *The Great Rebellion 1642–60*, London 1966.

Roskill, S., *The Navy at War 1939–45*, London 1961.

Round, J., *Geoffrey de Mandeville*, London 1892.

Salzmann, L., *Henry II*, London 1917.

Smith, G., *A History of England*, New York 1957.

Webb, E., *A History of the Twelfth Foot*, London 1914.

Western, J., *The English Militia in the 18th Century*, London 1965.

Whitelock, D., *The Anglo-Saxon Chronicle*, London 1961.

Willcox, W., *Portrait of a General: Sir Henry Clinton*, New York 1964.

Winbolt, S., *Britain Under the Romans*, London 1945.

Wood, D., *The Narrow Margin*, London 1961.

In addition the Victoria County Histories of Britain contain interesting material. The appropriate volumes are:

Cambridgeshire, edited by L. Salzmann, reprinted London 1962.

Essex, edited by W. Powell, reprinted London 1963.

Norfolk, edited by W. Page, London 1906.

Suffolk, edited by W. Page, London 1907.

Acknowledgements

The publishers are indebted to the following for permission to use illustrations: British Museum: pages 14, 27, 28, 49, 50. Cambridge University Collection: pages 10, 16–17, 19, 20–21, 35, 47, 81. Colchester and Essex Museum: pages 29, 30, 103, 105. The Department of the Environment: pages 12–13, 35, 40, 66–7, 70, 72, 74–5, 79, 82–3, 86, 87, 106, 119, 126. The Imperial War Museum: pages 136–7, 138, 139, 140–1, 142, 144–5, 146, 147. King's Lynn Museum and Art Gallery: page 99. The National Army Museum: pages 127, 132–3, 134–5. Radio Times–Hulton Picture Library: pages 24, 25, 26, 32–3, 34, 41, 42, 44, 45, 46, 56–7, 68–9, 77, 80, 84–5, 89, 90, 92–3, 94–5, 98, 100–1, 110–11, 113, 114–15, 122, 124–5, 128, 129.

The cover picture is of Orford Castle, Suffolk and is British Crown copyright; reproduced with the permission of the Controller of Her Britannic Majesty's Stationery Office.

INDEX

All numbers in italics refer to captions